MAKING AMERICAN
FOREIGN POLICY
in the
POLITICAL PRESSURE COOKER

MAKING AMERICAN FOREIGN POLICY

in the

POLITICAL PRESSURE COOKER

O. Lawrence Burnette, Jr.

**Formerly Research Professor of History in
Birmingham-Southern College
Sometimes Lecturer in History at the
University of West Florida**

To order additional copies of this book, contact:
Xlibris Corporation
1-888-795-4274
www.Xlibris.com
Orders@Xlibris.com
92421

CONTENTS

Dedicated with grateful thanks
to the
men and women
of the
American Armed Forces
who serve
to implement
American Foreign Policy

A NOTE TO THE READER

This little study addressing some of the recent and vexing foreign policy issues in American diplomacy was begun in the context of a Continuing Education class at the University of West Florida in the Winter-Spring of 2008 as the nation was undergoing the quadrennial exercise of another presidential election. The theme of the class was: 'Is a presidential campaign, the pressure cooker of American partisan politics, the preferred venue for making foreign policy?' Members of the class were a very mature group, with significant actual experience in the field of national security and foreign policy affairs, and they contributed many of the insights which may be found here. As always, the author alone is responsible for what bears his name.

The time and topic were deliberately chosen to catch the political winds then blowing through the nation. In that presidential election year most American citizens were vitally concerned about the various national security and foreign policy issues raised by the campaign, and in a sense the election was primarily a national plebiscite on the conflicts then raging in Iraq and Afghanistan. The rhetorical question raised for discussion was: 'Does the historical experience of the United States support the proposition that basic, long-term decisions in the field of foreign policy can or should be made in the heat of partisan campaigns?'

This volume does not pretend to be definitive history and to reach conclusive judgment. Instead, it seeks to use documentable historical analysis to provoke thought as to choices and decisions which must and will be made in response to some of the more weighty diplomatic and national security issues facing the United States in the post cold-war era. It is not remotely suggested that citizen participation in the on-going debates regarding foreign policy should be curtailed, however limited the factual information on which ultimate citizen decisions must be based. But is can be hoped that the more extreme partisanship which is sometimes employed primarily to secure the election of a given candidate or party may be mitigated by the sober, thoughtful participation of a better-informed and less partisan electorate. American politics may have become a blood sport, but mistakes in the area of foreign affairs are likely to be deadly.

The emphasis here is upon the process of reaching foreign policy decisions in a democratic society, one in which the direct power of the citizen is diluted by the very remoteness of actual policy determination from the political process and the manner in which presidents are chosen and discharge their constitutional foreign policy powers. In the American style of politics, domestic political, foreign policy and security issues are ground together in the sausage mill, not always with the proper regard for the long-term national best interests. Reflecting the author's experience and observations, he is concerned that foreign and security policies have at times been subjected to the baser aspects of party politics, especially in the period since the Spanish-American War. In a simpler and less-critical era, when the United States did not play a major role in world affairs, foreign policy questions did not generally engage the primary attention of the public. Was that an idyll whose time has simply passed? Nor is the author necessarily committed to the conclusions which may appear to being suggested here. These case studies are offered for sober reflection, discussion, and future decision-making on a more rational and objective basis.

Can American foreign policy be safely made in the political pressure cooker of presidential elections? On the answer to that question may hang the nature and the future of the Republic.

O. Lawrence Burnette, Jr.,
Lillian, on Perdido Bay, Alabama
Winter, 2011

CHAPTER 1

THE TRADITIONAL FOUNDATIONS OF AMERICAN FOREIGN POLICY: THE CONSTITUTIONAL AND POLITICAL CONSIDERATIONS IN MAKING FOREIGN POLICY

Politics is the science of resolving domestic state issues, but foreign policy should be about statesmanship. The two areas are certainly connected, but they are not the same thing—nor should the former drive the latter. In the formative years of the Republic, the two were more separate and distinct than has come to be case. In order to appreciate how far the nation has strayed from its traditional foreign policy, let us first look at the foundations of the traditional, historical American policy regarding the rest of the world.

American foreign policy until roughly the turn of the last century had been the result of rational study and analysis by experts in the classic American, or British, tradition—with a generous portion of good luck thrown in. Instead, following 1898 when the United States took its place as a world power, it has often become a political "wedge issue" in the on-going struggle between the two major parties. Neither has resisted the temptation to use foreign policy to gain political advantage. The result has been an inconsistent policy in which popular ends are either frustrated or misguided for ulterior or ideological political purposes. In that process the national best interests have often been miss-served or not properly calculated. In short, foreign policy differences of opinion have turned on narrow or transient issues. Those differences have at times resulted in the promotion of the short-term goals and the subversion of the true national interests.

Let us re-visit the historical roots of traditional American foreign policy. These policies were the basis for the protection and advancement of American national interests in the world outside our national borders.

1. "No entangling alliances." From George Washington forward, the proscription severed the young nation well. Of course, the prohibition on alliances was an outgrowth of our experience with the French alliance during and after the Revolutions—those of America and France. The prospect of going to war to defend the excesses of the French Revolution was so revolting that it formed the object lesson for the next century during which the nation was maturing. In America's adolescence, the world was a dangerous neighborhood for a constitutional republic, and a Swiss-like neutrality behind the safety of surrounding oceans served America well.

2. "Free ships make free trade" and "freedom of the seas" were more than pious slogans; they were also basic concepts employed by the nation when its commerce and independence was threatened by tensions and wars overseas. The new rules were a challenge to the traditional rules of international law, and America sought to establish the benefits of the change by force of its presumed moral superiority. To the degree that some nations supported the new doctrines, they advanced civility between those so observing, but it failed to keep us from armed conflict with Great Britain in 1812 when Britain steadfastly refused to comply. Throughout the nineteenth century there was a steady solidification of the doctrine of "might makes right," and by the time the United States became a world power it was ready to agree, even if the rough edges were smoothed for the American conscience.

3. "*De facto* recognition," the principle that whatever government actually rules a particular area was to be considered the legal government therein, was the steady policy of the United States until it was radically altered by President Wilson. In the place of long-established policy Wilson substituted the policy of "*de jure* recognition," by which the United States took to inquire as to the process by which a particular regime came to power. To what end was that new policy related to our national best interests? The

constitutional right of a president to establish such a rule is not questioned, but the practical result is open to debate. In addition to drawing America into foreign conflicts, it has not had the universal result desired by Wilson.

4. "Monroe Doctrine," the American announcement that the Western Hemisphere was closed to further European colonization, was neither essentially American, nor guaranteed by American power, and not generally appreciated in Latin America. It was, of course, conceived by Great Britain to advance its own interests, and when proposed as a joint statement America knew it would be enforced by the Royal Navy. Monroe stole the march by announcing the policy unilaterally. What American national best interests were served by the Doctrine, and at what price when it was no longer policed by British warships and when resented by neighbors in this hemisphere?

5. "No standing army and navy." It is axiomatic that a nation aspiring to power must have military power to project. Throughout the first century of independence, the United States adopted and consistently followed the policy of sustaining the smallest army and navy consistent with its limited goals and isolated position. The policy not only saved the Treasury, but it also saved national involvement in myriad international problems which might well have overwhelmed it. Nations which are not militarily prepared for war generally follow a more peaceful foreign policy, defending themselves through shrewd diplomacy rather than force of arms. On the other hand, large standing military force invites its occasional use just because it is available.

6. "Manifest Destiny," the concept that the nation was divinely appointed to achieve certain expansionist goals was the height of national arrogance, and that conclusion was not lost on the world powers. Who was appointed to discern the will of God, and how was the message to be authenticated? Adoption of the policy certainly did mobilize and seal the national purpose, but had it been directed against a first-rate power it would have resulted in national disaster. It is too clever by far seriously to suggest that the policy included the proviso that God was so disposed as to place only minor powers in the way of realization of that goal. Of course, the doctrine was invented by jingoes to morally justify their own view of the national future. It had

little to do with rational, national best interests, although it does seem to have worked out that way. Without the doctrine to cover national doubts, the national flag would not now be flying over the Louisiana Purchase, the Southwest, the Northwest, Alaska and Hawaii, and several islands of the Caribbean. Had American willpower been strong enough, the doctrine would have brought in Canada as well, but to what end? Was there no end to the desirable acquisition of land? American hearts may have swelled with pride at the notion that God Himself was directing the destiny (and expansion) of the nation, but were the results the result of national megalomania, as the rest of the world thought? The jury is still out on that question.

7. An open immigration policy and the promotion of democracy by the example of the American model were principles once deeply embedded in the national psyche. That America has closed the open door and pulled in the welcome mat seems almost a repudiation of the national personality.

8. Exactly where is American foreign policy made anyway? The obvious answer is in the State Department, but for purposes of argument indulge a bit of exaggeration for effect. The State Department was once the main engine for implementing if not making foreign policy, and it was lightly staffed by a few experts, somewhat independent of the president and whatever political goals he may have brought with him into office. Presidents, even those who are brilliant or who have had past experience in diplomacy, cannot know all things, and they rely upon advice and recommendations of experts in the State Department. The American process of diplomacy was based upon the British tradition of an elite corps doing what it had been trained to do, and beginning with Benjamin Franklin some remarkable individuals have held office unsung but effective in guiding the nation in troubled foreign waters. What can be said of the Department today? While the Secretary of State is the premier member of the cabinet, does he and his department actually make foreign policy, independent of the controlling influence of the Oval Office? There are ugly rumors that the Foreign Service has been reduced to the function of a glorified messenger service, ever a punching bag for opponents of the current foreign policy. When American embassies are as well staffed with operatives from

the Central Intelligence Agency and other intelligence branches, perhaps American interests in Moscow or Baghdad could be as well served by a Foreign Service code clerk, policy ultimately being made in Washington. If the Emperor really is naked, does it serve any purpose to pretend that he is clothed?

9. American foreign policy is ultimately the prerogative of one person, the president. The Constitutional authority to establish and direct foreign policy is clearly spelled out in the Constitution, Article II, Section 2(2): "He [the President] shall have power, by and with the consent of the Senate, to make treaties, provided two-thirds of the senators present concur and he shall nominate, and by and with advice of the Senate, shall appoint ambassadors, other public ministers and consuls, ..." That sweeping grant of power to the Executive, coupled with placing the military power to implement foreign policy in the same hands as contained in Section 2 (1): "The president shall be the commander in chief of the army and navy of the United States, and of the militia of the several states, when called into the actual service of the United States . . . ." These powers are plenary. Custom and circumstances may have broadened the presidential power in foreign affairs, but the balancing power of Congress to declare war and to appropriate funds for conducting foreign relations is still as binding today as when it was established. That being the case, for the sake of argument can a case be made that *all* foreign policy decisions made by the president in *all* cases must be accorded the presumption of constitutionality and in the national interest, overriding contrary opinion of the people as expressed by polls or by their representatives in Congress? On occasion that question has been hotly debated, and perhaps it should be finally decided by the Supreme Court. This is not to suggest that foreign policy should be made at the ballot box, but that foreign policy should be but one of the mix of issues involved in the political process.

10. The United States as a young nation took the lead in promoting international good will, in protecting the international rights of all peoples and nations, in advocating copyrights and postal service internationally, and in suppressing the slave trade. America was a shining beacon of human hope in a world ruled by great nations wielding absolute power. American embassies were once havens of sanctuary, to which victims of persecution could repair to seek

shelter and protection. Today, such victims are more likely to encounter a bunker mentality and an armed Marine Corps sentry. While the United States has certainly contributed to this change mind set, are its national best interests served by outright hatred by large portions of the world population? The homes of several European heads of state are not even symbolically guarded, because no one seems to consider the threat real or creditable. What has caused American symbols to become such inviting targets in the modern world?

11. Prior to about 1890 the stress upon American foreign policy from competing special interests was held to a minimum; not because they did not exist, but because they were effectively resisted. More recently special interests have learned how to mobilize an under-informed public opinion to pressure foreign policy to serve its will. Is the national best interests thereby served?

12. The tariff occupied a great deal of political attention in an earlier day, because it was at the juncture of foreign and domestic policy. The North desired high tariffs to protect its emerging industries; the South favored European goods and needed to sell its cotton to buy them, therefore it favored a low tariff. That sectional dispute in part was a cause of the Civil War, but once that unpleasantness was over high tariffs became the rule. Later generations of special economic interests learned from past experience how to shape tariff policy to their own special ends.

13. Viewed through the long lens of history, American foreign policy prior to about 1890 was a remarkable success. It kept America safe in an increasingly dangerous world, and it permitted the United States to mature unmolested, true to its Revolutionary principles. Only once, in the War of 1812, was America dragged into an un-welcome international conflict, and that was probably caused by the failure of Britain to accept American independence as a result of the Revolution. Even so, despite having effectively lost the war, American diplomacy was able to negotiate an honorable peace. Foreign policy was clear and consistent throughout the first century of American independence, not fodder for political campaigns, shaped by political leaders which history has judged as statesmen. Was America incredibly lucky, or did it foresee and avoid the dangers of allowing divisive foreign policy issues to be subjected to partisan debate?

When diplomatic historians go looking to discern the relative successes of American foreign policy, they are often forced to conclude that a consistent and rational policy has been lacking since the turn of the last century. Instead, what they usually find more closely resembles a drunken sailor, stumbling down the street, unsure of where he is going or of what purpose, yet certain in his own foggy mind that he is on the right path home. Such a sailor also rues the next day after he sobers up.

Given the fundamental shifts in America's role in the modern world, it is perhaps unfair to expect the simplicity and rationality of an earlier day to govern the formulation of foreign policy. But it is equally unfair, even mortally dangerous, to attempt to make foreign policy in the vortex of presidential campaigns if the result is the polarization of public opinion about the fundamental direction of foreign policy? Is it too much to ask a democracy to debate such life-or-death issues in the off years when not preoccupied about choosing a president to implement the agreed-upon direction? Among the presidential functions anticipated by the Constitution was the preparation of public opinion for the perceived need to engage in war, and that process has not always been followed.

That having been proposed, how does the American public exercise its democratic rights to self-determination when confronted by presidential authority determined to follow an unpopular course in foreign affairs? Is withholding of appropriations or impeachment the only recourse? That, of course, raises a national danger of its own. "Quickie" wars (or police actions), which do not generally accomplish ill-defined goals or enjoy overwhelming public support, have forced America to endure recently a series of such experiences. Their costs in human blood and national treasure are the same as those which are declared wars. Other than insisting upon an objective awareness of what is at issue when the nation commits itself to armed conflict can constitutional democracy be made to function as intended. How is that to be done and still speak with one voice to the world at large?

In the final analysis, foreign policy is not a game in which only those chosen to lead may play. Nor is it a subject to be blindly trusted to the good sense of those who are elected. It would be extremely beneficial if foreign policy issues could be debated outside normal political contests, and once a basic agreement is reached for it to be clothed with the toga of non-partisanship unless radically altered circumstances demand radical surgery. It is too important to be left to political chance.

While the United States was learning its way in the world of diplomacy, the rest of the world looked on with a mixture of wry amusement and wonder. Perhaps Otto von Bismarck, Chancellor of Germany, spoke for most European leaders when he observed, "There is an all-wise God who looks after fools, drunkards, and the United States of America."

CHAPTER 2

IMPERIAL EXPANSION AT THE TURN OF THE TWENTIETH CENTURY

Although there had been a few attempts at overseas expansion before 1898, in that year the situation in Cuba provided the ideal impetus. In the years preceding, the ideology of expansion had been growing, and it had already been realized by the acquisition of Hawaii and the Virgin Islands, and only personal conflicts had prevented the annexation of Santo Domingo in the heady years of Republican Party domination in the 1870's. America was flexing its muscles, waiting for the right moment to express itself. That moment came in the Cuban crisis of 1898.

Cuba had long been of serious interest to American expansionists, and since it was so close to American shores some thought it was covered by Manifest Destiny. The rebellion of the Cubans against Spain was seized upon with ulterior motives, and the crisis was fanned into a war of convenience with Spain, with fateful consequences for the future destiny of the United States. It is true that the Cuban rebels sought to capitalize on American interest in their homeland to draw the United States into their struggle against Spain. But in asking the United States to save them from Spanish rule, they wound up exchanging Spanish for American colonialism, and loosed upon the world a new imperial power as a bonus. Stirred by the opportunity to promote American trade interests, Senator John Tyler Morgan of Alabama urged President McKinley to "dispatch a fleet of warships to Cuba," whether to help the Cuban rebels or to take Cuba for ourselves was not made exactly clear. He was joined by Joseph Pulitzer and William Randolph; their goal was to sell newspapers, but the result was to whip American public opinion into a frenzy, which exploded into war—which further resulted in the acquisition of territory far removed from Cuba and having nothing whatever to do with the conditions on that island. Once the opportunity was presented, all manner of interests joined in the clamor of war. Even the Protestant Evangelical churches were infected with war fever. It became a case of imperialism with a religion as justification.

Complicated international conferences ensued, with the European powers seeking to shield Spain from humiliation by America, and the United States openly resisted such pressures because it had ulterior motives to serve. In the end, a lack of consensus among the European powers doomed Spain to its fate. Time and again as American reporters sought by inflamed reports from Cuba to justify American intervention, the resulting cabled response from their editors would reveal the true state of things: "You supply the news. We will supply the war."

American involvement came a giant step forward with the destruction of the USS *Maine* in Havana harbor. A naval court of inquiry investigated the cause of the destruction of the ship and the loss of 260 members of the crew. The finding was that the cause was an external mine, without attempting to fix the guilty party. American public opinion and the press had no such difficulty, and Spanish treachery was loudly proclaimed. The Navy, presumably under Executive orders, hauled the hulk out to sea and sank it in the depths of the Caribbean, foreclosing any future examination of the wreckage. Aroused public opinion did not need to retry the case, and it demanded retaliation and vengeance. War hysteria was rampant, and although not all political leaders were so inclined, the possible political advantages to be gained by capitalizing on the circumstances was not lost to the more expansionist minded. The senior member of the Senate Foreign Relations Committee, George Frisby Hoar, decried the rush to action and to war, but he was ignored as one who had outlived his days. President McKinley diddled and allowed the war sentiment to fester. On the ostensible basis that Spain had failed acceptably to respond to the American demand to resolve the Cuban crisis, the President finally asked for a resolution from Congress allowing the use of armed force.

The Assistant Secretary of the Navy, Theodore Roosevelt, hell-bent to taste the spoils of war, confided to a friend, "We here in Washington have grown to feel that almost every man connected with the big business interests of the country is anxious to court any infamy if only peace can be obtained and the business situation be not disturbed." Those same business leaders in 1898 were more concerned with recovery from the depression of 1893 than they were in overseas expansion, but they would be led to understand that expansion would cure the recurring ills of business cycles. That same Teddy Roosevelt, while acting Secretary of the Navy in the absence of the Secretary, cabled Commodore George Dewey at Hong Kong to load coal and steam *post haste* to the Philippine Islands to be in a situation to confront units of the Spanish Navy stationed there. The Philippines had nothing to do with the situation in Cuba, but Cuba provided the excuse to put in operation the "large policy" which naval and some political leaders had been just waiting for.

If war were to come, best it be made to be worthwhile. President McKinley piously washed his hands, appealing to "a duty to humanity" and asked the Congress for a declaration of war. He knew that had he not done so, Congress would have so responded anyway, and possibly moved to impeach him in the bargain. McKinley, not totally honest with himself or with the American people, later plead, "I did all that in honor could be done to avert war, but without avail."

The parallel with the run-up to the conflict in Iraq in 2003 is eerie.

The war which ensued was a "splendid little war," to quote Secretary of State John Hay. "[It was] begun with the highest motives, carried on with magnificent intelligence and spirit, and favored by that Fortune which loves the brave." As Commodore Dewey prepared to reduce the Spanish fleet in Manila Bay to rubble before breakfast, he laconically informed a staff officer, "You may fire when ready, Gridley." And later during the destruction of the Spanish fleet, "Don't cheer boys, the poor devils are dieing." The war was begun in the spirit of daring-do as if nothing could go wrong—but it did. The Army was totally ill-prepared, and despite a courageous charge up San Juan Hill by the Rough Riders led by Lieutenant-Colonel Theodore Roosevelt (who traded his Assistant Secretary's desk for an Army uniform and became an American popular hero), the army did not cover itself with glory. General Nelson Miles led his famous "Moonlight expedition to capture Puerto Rico," and the American fleet sent to re-enforce Dewey stopped off along the way to pick off Guam. American soldiers suffered as much from Yellow Fever as they did from Spanish bullets, and they ate "embalmed beef" left over from the Indian wars of the 1870's, but still and all an American empire was being collected. In fact, the most pressing problem after the quick conflict was over was what to do with the spoils, or particularly with the Philippine Islands.

Just after the Battle of Manila Bay, Commodore Dewey received aboard his flagship the native leader of the Philippine insurrection, General Emilio Aguinaldo, with ceremony befitting the head of a sovereign power. General Aguinaldo later swore that the Commodore promised him independence for the islands, but the Commodore swore that he made no such promises. In any event, there is in the Commodore's private correspondence a personal note from Secretary of the Navy Long criticizing the naval officer for exceeding his authority in dealing at all with the native leader. Dewey was already an American hero, so it was done in private and with a kid glove. "You should not have done that without consulting higher authority," admonished the Secretary, so the admiring public never knew that their hero had been dressed down. The Commodore was promoted to Admiral and was brought home in glory to receive a jeweled sword from Congress on behalf of a grateful nation—and quietly retired.

The problem of justifying the peace terms back home proved to be even more troublesome than the war which won the spoils. After the flush of patriot fever had subsided, there began to be murmurs about the probable results of rushing into imperialistic expansion. In what seems to have been an unseemly haste, peace commissioners, including four senators (excluding Senator Hoar), were sent to Paris to dictate terms to the Spanish. Spain readily agreed to independence for Cuba (even agreeing to assume the Cuban debt contracted while a colony), and the cession of Puerto Rico and Guam, but it balked at the demand for the Philippines on the grounds that they had not been conquered in war. While that issue was being debated in Paris, a similar debate was going on at home. Several organs of the Protestant Evangelical movement swung behind cession of the islands in order to do God's work, even confessing support for "imperialism for righteousness," and the Presbyterian Church resolved that America should take the islands as a "necessary part of the great outward impulse of civilization, the missionary movement welcomes as an ally." The Chicago *Times-Herald*, usually a paper reflecting the views of the McKinley Administration editorialized: "We find that we want the Philippines . . . . The people now believe that the United States owes it to civilization to accept the responsibilities imposed upon it by the fortunes of war." Mindful of its fellow Catholic Philippine members, the Catholic Church in America loudly protested, but its pleas were brushed aside in the mad dash to gain empire. In other words, in the Philippines (the most Christian area in the Orient) the White Man's Burden was assumed on behalf of God and civilization. If the United States could turn a profit from owning them, so much the better.

The American public was not yet fully supportive of rounding out the new empire by annexing the Philippines, so the President said that he asked Almighty God for guidance. Speaking to a group of visiting Methodist clergymen he related, "One night late it came to me this way . . . . (1) That we could give them back to Spain—that would be cowardly and dishonorable; (2) that we could not turn them over to France or Germany—our commercial rivals in the Orient—that would be bad business and discreditable; (3) that we could not leave them to themselves—they were unfit for self-government—and they would soon have anarchy and misrule over there worse than Spain's was; and (4) that there was nothing left to do but take them all, and to educate the Filipinos, and uplift them; Christianize them. I went to bed . . . and slept soundly." General Aguinaldo must have been surprised to learn that God had instructed the American President make his country an American colony, and he reacted by declaring a bloody rebellion against the American occupation, which unfortunately was seriously marred by incidents of American torture, including "water boarding." The rebellion went on for about ten years before it was finally put down. To salve the American conscience, McKinley offered Spain an indemnity of several million dollars for the islands, which she sullenly accepted.

In the aftermath, poets on both sides of the annexation question had a field day. Rudyard Kipling, the British favorite who strongly supported America adopting an imperial policy, wrote these lines:

> Take up the White Man's burden—
> Send forth the best ye breed—
> Go bind your sons to exile
>
> To serve your captives' needs;
> To wait in heavy harness,
> "Ron fluttered folk and wild—
> Your new-caught, sullen people,
> Half devil and half-child.

Rather poor poetry," snickered Roosevelt, "but good sense from the expansionist standpoint."

On the other side of public opinion, William Vaughan Moody wrote for the aroused conscience of the nation, deeply bothered by the winds which were converting America from a republic into an empire.

> Lies! Lies! It cannot be! The wars we wage
> Are noble, and our battles still are won
> By justice for us, ere we lift the gage.
> We have not sold our loftiest heritage.
> The proud republic hath not stooped to clear
> And scramble in the market-place of war . . . .
> Ah no!
> We have not fallen so.

Better poetry, perhaps, but definitely in the minor key of prevailing public opinion, so quickly was it changing.

As the war spirit slowly gave way, many who had of late so strongly supported war for foreign gain now bowed their heads in shame. The Democratic senators and a sizable number of their Republican colleagues declared their misgivings and some their outright opposition. Sensing an opening for partisan advantage, more and more Democratic politicians began to point out the inconsistency of America having secured her independence by revolting against an empire now adopting the policy of imperialism. William Jennings Bryan, the last Democratic candidate for President, declared his opposition to the Treaty of Paris and arranged to have the Democratic platform in 1900 declare that "any government not based on the consent of the people is tyranny." McKinley for the Republican expansionists answered, "Do we need their consent to perform a great act of charity?" When other Republicans demanded to know who would be so craven as to haul down the flag over the Philippines, Bryan returned the favor by asking who would be brave enough to haul down the President? Beginning with this unfortunate exchange, the American public has been caught in a cross-fire of competing brands of patriotism. It has often become a 'hot button' in political competition when other issues fail to capture public attention. It may be noted that "super-patriotism" often hides some form of ulterior political motive, a corollary to Dr. Samuel Johnson's dictum that patriotism is the last refuge of a scoundrel. When citizens of a republic reach for motive and question opponents' patriotism in debates about foreign policy, the republic (whether it be Greek, Roman, or American) is in danger.

Mark Hanna, the Republican boss from Ohio, sought to quell some of the public dissent regarding the departure upon an imperial policy in the election of 1900 by engineering the nomination of the war hero, Theodore Roosevelt, as Vice-President. Shortly after the election McKinley was shot in Buffalo, N. Y., and Roosevelt escalated to the White House. When Hanna heard the news, he exclaimed, "That madman the President of the United States? Good God!" In a matter of a few months the first great public debate about American foreign policy became an accomplished fact, the new President having been one of those who had promoted and engineered the transformation. Once the policy of empire was established, it took time for the milk of actual experience to curdle and sour.

In the Senate the Treaty of Paris had rough going, finally being approved by just one vote over the required two-thirds majority. Both Republicans and Democrats voted for and against the Treaty, but the die was cast; the Republican Party took on the mantle of expansionism and protecting national security, while the Democrats howled in the wilderness. America went on to become the master of the Caribbean and a player on the Asian scene, to what ends and related to which national best interests? The Navy loved its elevated role and the new money for ships and manpower it brought. Captain Alfred T. Mahan, the Navy's schoolmaster at the Naval War College, wrote and published his seminal study on *The Influence of Seapower upon History*, which became the Navy's doctrinal handbook on the reason for its expanded existence as the handmaiden of imperialism. The nation felt the thrill of national pride, convincing itself that expanding the scope of American influence in world affairs was the proper badge of office as well as serving God's will. Politicians promoted Admirals, Admirals ordered new ships, business profited from such ship orders, American steelworkers had steady work, and workmen voted for Republican candidates, who promised to perpetuate the cycle. The military-industrial complex about which President Eisenhower warned was born in the aftermath of the Spanish-American War.

American businessmen were also blinded by the vision of selling millions of Chinese those American products being made in excess of domestic needs. But they forgot that one of the basic premises of capitalism is that potential customers must have money before they can pay for their purchases. Instead, as to trade with China, it worked the other way around, China sending boatloads of consumer goods to fill American orders, thereby converting Chinese Communism into a form of capitalism. It is also well to remember that the Philippines were an early target for Japanese expansionism in 1941, and America paid dearly in defending the putative American interests in Asia from which there has been so little return. Subic Bay Naval Base and Clark Field in the Philippines may have played vital roles in the Vietnamese conflict, but without being invested in those bases America would have had far less reason for entering the conflict in the first place. Nations sometimes defend that which they already control and hope to develop, without necessarily referring to the changing calculus of foreign affairs. It is the function of statesmen to discern what is and what is not vital to national interests. The United States was lacking statesmen in the fateful turn of events surrounding the War with Spain, and it has paid the price ever since. American imperialist expansion as a policy was adopted in haste, without adequate debate, and certainly not in an impartial, objective environment in which the advantages and disadvantages could be weighed. In the last analysis, it was done in large measure to advance partisan advantage.

Perhaps Homer, the Greek statesman and poet, had it right when he observed, "He serves his party best who serves his country best."

CHAPTER 3

WOODROW WILSON AND THE LEAGUE OF NATIONS DEBATE

Woodrow Wilson was born in a Presbyterian parsonage, and he never got over that fact. His high-minded idealism, unwillingness to compromise on practical political issues, and his prophetic vision may have made him an excellent Professor of Political Science. In fact, he is the only President who has come to office with that kind of educational preparation. At once, that made him ideally suited to lead the world back from the excesses of imperialism, but it also made him an unlikely candidate for politician of the year. He did not understand the mind set of the American people, and they did not understand his lofty idealism. His speeches read like university lectures, and although he was one of the most influential of American presidents when viewed through the perspective of history, in his own day he must be counted as something of a political failure. In fact, the single issue most dear to his heart was the creation of a League of Nations, and he failed to secure the co-operation of his own country because of his ineptness as a political leader. He provided brilliant leadership to the nation in fighting World War I; he bullied the seasoned leaders of Europe into agreeing with his lofty view of world order; yet he could not sell his ideas at home. He was an accomplished political leader, yet he lacked charisma. From his Scottish ancestors came his stubbornness and self-righteousness. Had he been able to deal exclusively with domestic issues, he might have left an even more impressive record of social, political, and economic reform, but when he strayed into the field of foreign affairs, he was out of his element.

Wilson chose a troubled time in which to be President. America was ambivalent about its new role in world affairs, and as storm clouds were gathering over Europe as the two contending power blocks competed and prepared for war, Wilson simultaneously desired to keep the United States out of the conflict but also be in position to mold the post-war world. In the role of international policeman, the United States had intervened in the Dominican Republic to keep several European powers from doing so, and America had extended a protectorate over Haiti when revolution threatened to unhinge the fragile stability of the Caribbean. Some American leaders had assumed that such a function was expandable to the whole world.

The election of 1908 in large measure turned upon the troubling issues of foreign policy, and those issues lay at the root of the election of 1912 when the Republican opposition was split between the positions of Roosevelt and his hand-picked successor, William Howard Taft. Taft had disgusted Roosevelt by his failure aggressively to seize upon the imperialist opportunities, thereby failing to insure American security, now tied to expansionism, and Republican dominance in the field of foreign affairs.

Upon becoming President in 1913, Wilson was forced to accept William Jennings Bryan, former standard bearer of the Democratic Party, as Secretary of State—and American foreign policy promptly suffered from a lack of clear policy. Bryan had little experience in foreign affairs, but he sought to impose his views of international order and morality upon an even more moralistic President, who had more than enough of those traits. Relations between the White House and the State Department suffered, and in desperation Wilson appointed Colonel Edward M. House as his personal agent for foreign relations. House was a Texas millionaire who had made his fortune in international trade, a sort of earlier-day James Baker, but of the Democratic persuasion. The nation was well served by having his advice, but the usual channels of making and implementing policy through the State Department broke down.

With House's help, Wilson sought to stem the rising tide of anti-American sentiment in Latin America by creating the Pan-American Union, a regional test model for the League of Nations to be projected at a later date. It died aborning.

Not totally immune from imperial fever, Wilson himself took advantage of the imminent threat to Denmark from the looming war in Europe by purchasing the Virgin Islands for $25 million dollars. It was justified as an insurance policy to protect the Panama Canal, but a casual glance at the map suggests other motives may have been operating. Besides, there were already other American bases strategically guarding the canal.

Another vexing problem in foreign policy facing Wilson was the unrest in Mexico. There a revolution had broken out in 1911, led by the youthful reformer, Francisco Madero, who ousted the dictator, Porfirio Diaz. But in the age-old pattern of revolutions, this one overran itself when Madero's general, Victoriano Huerta, betrayed his chief and led a counter-revolution against Madero.

When Wilson took office in 1913 he inherited the tangled mess in Mexico, and he decided that the key to the solution was in replacing Huerta. In turn, Huerta responded defiantly by proclaiming, "I will resist with arms any attempt by the United States to interfere with the affairs of Mexico." After laying the whole web in the lap of Congress, Wilson fumed over what to do next. He first tried to get the British to issue a joint statement, but the Royal Navy needed Mexican oil so that went nowhere. Then Wilson declared an embargo on arms going to the Huerta regime. Tensions reached the boiling point when a group of sailors from the USS *Dolphin* went ashore at Tampico to buy some gasoline and were arrested. Although an apology was quickly issued to Admiral Henry T. Morgan, commanding the Caribbean squadron, the President decided the use the incident as a pretext to force Huerta from office. Upon orders from "higher authority," the Admiral demanded a twenty-one gun salute to the American flag, thus converting a petty local incident into an international crisis. With his national pride aroused, Huerta demanded a return salute, gun for gun. Moreover, the American Atlantic Fleet was ordered to Tampico, as were several French and British naval vessels. The London *Times* soberly chided the American President for a "return to medieval conditions, a sad day for civilization." Fortunately, Huerta resigned before the matter got completely out of hand, but the domestic chaos in Mexico brought new threats in the form of raids across the border by bandits led by Pancho Villa. Such raids continued for several weeks, ultimately being suppressed by an expedition into Mexico led by General John J. Perishing (thereby giving him experience and public exposure as the American field commander when the United States entered World War I in 1917).

The conflict which was already raging in Europe posed a much greater threat to America than the affair with Mexico, yet the President's mind as focus elsewhere. "Do you think the glory of America would be enhanced by a war of conquest with Mexico?' Wilson confided in his diary. Soon afterward, the Pershing expedition was recalled, a new constitution was written for Mexico, and Wilson was happy to extend *de jure* recognition to the Mexican regime. Because it was so badly handled, the crisis with Mexico almost derailed the nation and its president just as they were about to be drawn into the war in Europe.

Woodrow Wilson learned from sad experience that "points of honor" do not always justify a nation going to war. There is a clear distinction between wars of convenience and those involving vital national interests.

*   *   *

Blood is thicker than water, and as it is with families, so it is with nations. In the conflict which raged in Europe from 1915, American sympathies were clearly with Britain and France and against Germany and Austria. The echoes of French aid during the American Revolution tugged at America's heartstrings, and a popular poem carefully caught the sentiment of the moment:

> Give us a name to fill the mind
> With stirring thoughts that lead mankind,
>
> A name like a star, a name of light,
> I give you *France.*

The polyglot national origins of the American people was caught in the crossfire of competing propaganda for one side or the other. Americans of Irish or German ancestry generally favored the Central Powers, while everyone else generally cheered the Allies. The American President issued the declaration of neutrality, but he went on to advise his countrymen to "be impartial in thought as well as in action."

The scholar and statesman that was Wilson expected both sides to respect established international law regarding the rights of neutrals and their trade—and their ships. But the new, total war brought new tactics, blowing away the old laws respecting the conduct of war. Both sides declared a naval blockade against the other, with new weapons (including submarines) to enforce it, which directly violated American neutral rights.

Britain suffered more on balance, because she was more dependent on American trade. Wall Street bankers loaned vast sums with which to prosecute the war, and Germany suffered more from being cut off from war supplies and food. British violations were not as blatant as those of Germany, so the American government looked the other way. Sir Cecil Spring-Rice, the British Ambassador in Washington, privately cabled his Foreign Office: "All the State Department are on our side except Bryan, who is incapable of forging a settled judgment on anything outside of party politics. The President will be with us by birth and upbringing."

Had the Central Powers been able to win in a lightening war, as they planned in the Schlieffen Plan, the outcome would have favored that side. As it degenerated into a protracted trench warfare on the Western Front, a war of attrition favored the Allies—because of the ultimate possibility of American involvement. Germany, after much backing and filling, decided to go for broke and use unrestricted submarine warfare against merchant shipping. The moralist in Wilson reacted with outrage, but Secretary Bryan insisted that Americans traveling on belligerent ships did so at their own risk. Wilson took a stand in favor of traditional rights of neutrals and insisted that American traveling on *any* ship, neutral or belligerent, be protected in their right to do so. What Wilson conveniently overlooked was the settled doctrine that passengers on any vessel of whatever flag were supposed to look to the flag of that nation for protection.

Fully aware of the divided public opinion in the United States, when Germany in 1915 resumed unrestricted submarine warfare, it took out ads in some 50 American newspapers warning of the dangers of travel on Allied vessels. When the British Cunard liner, *Luisitania*, fatefully sailed from New York with about 200 Americans aboard—and 4,200 cases of rifle cartridges for the British Army, it sailed into mortal danger. On May 7, 1915, just off the Irish coast, a German U-boat without warning sank the liner with the loss of 1,198 lives, including many women and children. "The nation which remembered the *Maine* will not forget the civilians of the *Luisitania!*" screamed the New York *Tribune*. "There is such a thing as a man being too proud to fight," replied Wilson. But the American President was determined to force Germany to accept the consequences of its violation of the rules of warfare, so he drafted a stern note to Germany, which forced Bryan to resign rather than sign it. Without the moderating influence of Bryan, Wilson demanded that Germany pay an indemnity for the loss of life, and give up unrestricted submarine warfare for the remainder of the war. Wilson's note concluded that the Unites States was "contending for nothing less high and sacred than the right of humanity."

Germany bowed to American pressure, promising to reign in its use of submarines without warning, but it continued to attack both Allied and American ships headed to Great Britain. In defense of the policy of his government German Chancellor Count Bethmann-Hollweg declared, "I cannot concede a humbling of Germany and the German people, or wresting of the submarine weapon from our hands."

On-rushing events carried the United States ever closer into the war. Representative Jeff McLemore of Texas and Senator Thomas P. Gore of Oklahoma drafted a resolution withdrawing American protection from American civilians traveling on belligerent ships, and Congress seemed ready to pass the measure. Wilson countered with a claim of Executive Power by signing an open letter that he "could not consent to any abridgment of the rights of American citizens in any respect." In full exercise of his constitutional authority Wilson addressed a new note to Germany: "Unless the Imperial Government should now immediately declare and effect and abandonment of its present methods of submarine warfare against passenger and freight-carrying vessels, the Government of the United States can have no choice but to sever diplomatic relations with the Government of the German Empire altogether."

Faced with the real threat of conflict with the United States, the German civilian leadership backed down—one last time—and issued the so-called *Sussex* pledge, by which it promised that German submarines would obey international law if the United States would similarly compel the British to lift their blockade on foodstuffs against Germany and her allies. Shrewd as Wilson could be, he accepted the pledge but failed to acknowledge the proviso. Having gained the upper hand in the match with Germany, the British took aggressive action to tighten their blockade as well as action against the Irish rebels supporting Germany, as well as blacklisting American ships suspected of trading with Germany. Wilson wrote in his diary, "I am . . . about at the end of my patience with Great Britain and the Allies. This blacklisting business is the last straw." He asked for and got Congressional authority to use force to compel all powers to respect American neutrality.

"Everybody seems to want peace," Wilson mused in his diary, "but nobody is willing to concede enough to get it." So he sent Colonel House to sound out the leaders in London, Paris, and Berlin on the possibilities of a peaceful end of the war. The Colonel returned convinced that the country would soon be at war, and he advised the President to prepare for it.

Early in 1916 Wilson determined to try for peace one last time, and he again sent House to Europe with the charge to merely reach a stalemate, in which the United States would act as a mediator to dictate the terms of peace to both sides. In the resulting House-Grey Memorandum, Britain agreed that whenever it and France thought the time "opportune", they would invite the United States and its Professor-President to teach Europe how to make peace. The Memorandum also included a provision that if the Central Powers refused the invitation, the United States would "probably" enter the war on the side of the Allies.

With such a peace plan in hand, in 1916 President Wilson went to the American voters for re-election with the slogan, "He kept us out of war." The Republican Party passed over Theodore Roosevelt, who was in serious contention as the leader of the nation which would *force* the end of the war or join it—and nominated Justice Charles Evans Hughes of the Supreme Court. Although there was no essential difference between the positions of Wilson and Hughes on the war in Europe, the Democratic Party sealed the deal with a clever advertising campaign featuring such ads as:

You are Working—*Not Fighting!*
Alive and Happy—*Not Cannon Fodder!*
or
Wilson with Peace with Honor?
Hughes and Roosevelt and War?

The German Ambassador in Washington reported to Berlin, "If Hughes is defeated he has only Roosevelt to thank for it."

Wilson did win re-election, and the Germans read correctly the tea leaves—announcing on December 12 that they were willing to discuss peace with the Allies. Actually, neither side was willing to discuss peace with the other, and certainly not in an international conference hosted by Wilson. Stymied, the President went before the Senate to explain what he had in mind and to mobilize public opinion in support of it. Declaring that there must be a "peace without victory," because a defeat of Germany would not be permanent, Wilson insisted upon "a peace made securely by the organized major force of mankind." In other words, one way or another, he intended to create the League of Nations.

Against the moral force which Wilson sought to mobilize, Germany again decided to gamble on all-out victory; it resumed unrestricted submarine warfare effective February 11, 1917. The German generals had decided to pass the last hope of victory to the German admirals and their submarines. As expected, Wilson broke diplomatic relations with Germany, but he assured Congress that only "actual overt acts" would cause him to seek a declaration of war.

While waiting to see what Germany would actually do, the State Department received from the British an intercepted copy of the famous Zimmerman Telegram, in which the German Minister in Mexico was instructed to ask if that country might be interested in making war on the United States in the event they entered the European contest. Mexico would be compensated by the re-acquisition of the "lost territories" of California, Arizona, New Mexico, and Texas. When the telegram was published a few days later is created a storm. Mexico was no real threat to the United States, but most Americans were ready to fight a nation which would stoop to such craven tactics.

In response to Wilson's request for additional support and authority, Congress authorized him to arm merchant vessels, an action resisted by "a little group of willful men" led by Senators Robert LaFollette and George W. Norris. They filibustered the bill to death, so Wilson took the action by Executive Order. Very promptly, three American ships were lost, including many American lives. "If the United States is to make good its word, it must go to war," opined the Chicago *Daily Tribune*. Most Americans agreed.

A president who leads a divided nation into war does so at his own peril. Wilson's sole concession to the resistance to war was to insist that America was in a separate fight, *together* with the Allies, but *not* joining them. That important distinction if not a difference was to have an important bearing on the peace negotiations after the war.

*   *   *

About the same time that America was entering the war, the Boleshivik Party in Russia was leading that troubled country out of the war and into a separate peace—and also into a protracted civil war between Communists and Czarists so memorably chronicled in the novel and movie, "Dr. Zhivago." By retiring from the conflict Russia hoped to escape total ruin and to establish a base from which to export Communism to the world at large. By doing so, however, it released millions of German soldiers from the Eastern Front for service in the West, and the French and British were earnestly scrambling for immediate help. That help came in the American army, led by General John J. Pershing. Upon arriving in France, he went to Lafayette's tomb to announce, "Lafayette, nous'avon ici." (Lafayette, we are here.) Over two million American troops followed him to France, to engage in some of the bloodiest conflict ever fought, anywhere.

Back in Washington, while feverishly seeking to mobilize America for the war, Wilson was also working on the peace plan to follow, to guarantee the peace. Lenin and the Communists were not impressed. Partially correct, they thought that the United States was still an imperial power seeking to extend its power, the chief obstacle to communizing the world community.

Wilson's post-war peace plan was popularly known as the Fourteen Points, and they provided the following:

1. The end of secret diplomacy.
2. Freedom of navigation on the seas in peace as well as in war.
3. Removal of the barriers to international free trade.
4. Reduction of armaments.
5. Impartial adjustment of colonial claims, taking into account the welfare of colonial peoples.
6. German evacuation of Russian territory and welcoming Russia "into the society of free nations under institutions of her own choosing." (But Russia was to cease fomenting revolution.)
7. German evacuation of Belgium and restoration of her sovereignty.
8. Return of Alsace-Lorraine to France, taken in 1871 by Prussia.
9. Readjustment of Italy's frontiers according to nationality.
10. Autonomy for the diverse peoples of the Austro-Hungarian Empire.
11. Rearrangement of the boundaries for nationalities under Turkish rule and free passage through the Dardanelles for ships of all nations.
12. Rearrangement of boundaries of the Balkan countries according to nationality.
13. An independent Poland with free access to the sea.
14. A general association of nations (i.e., The League of Nations).

Casual review of the Fourteen Points suggests that they went far beyond solving the immediate causes of World War I. Collectively, they were nothing less than a charter for a new World Order, one in which "good order and discipline" (a fine old Presbyterian phrase) would establish and maintain the peace of the world through moral force mobilized by the United States of America. It was breath-taking in the scope of concept. The academic in Wilson could have been expected to author nothing less.

The Allies were delighted to have the Fourteen Points as counterweights to German peace plans, even if they never intended to carry them into practice. Neither was Lenin impressed with Wilson's ideal of world peace. "The interests of socialism are above the right of a nation to self-determination," he declared. So Russia swallowed the bitter pill of the Treaty of Brest-Litovsk in order to secure as much as possible the freedom of Communism to become rooted and expand. During the fighting in Europe the United States sent an army to Siberia to help keep that part of the Russian empire from falling into Communist hands, but about the only accomplishments were exposing thousands of American troops to frostbite and alcoholism. The Russians still have a bone to pick with the United States about that intervention.

There is no evidence to prove that the Fourteen Points had any effect upon the German army's will to fight to Allies to a final resolution. Re-enforced by hundreds of thousands from the Eastern Front, the Germans became an even more stubborn foe. Under the over-all command of Marshal Foch, the Allied armies gradually forced the German army back to the border, and to a *status quo ante bellum*. In the world's most catastrophic war to that date, exhausted and short of food and supplies, the German army finally surrendered on November 11, 1918. Hundreds of thousands of American troops found their final rest in graves in France, and thousands more brought home their wounds of the war.

American public opinion on the Fourteen Points was mixed and provided plenty of political issues for years to come. The victorious Allies had grave reservations, but they bided their time. Theodore Roosevelt and Senator Henry Cabot Lodge, the senior Republican expert in foreign policy, attacked the plan as too soft on the vanquished. "Let us dictate peace with hammering guns," thundered Roosevelt. Even some of the senior Democratic senators were concerned, so when Wilson made a direct appeal to the voters to make the election of 1918 a referendum on the League and all it stood for, the tactic backfired. The voters elected a Republican Congress by a narrow margin. Perhaps they did not know what they were doing, or with what long-term results.

Most Americans assumed in 1918 that the defeat of Germany would usher in an era of business as usual, bringing the boys home, and allowing Europe to stew in its own juice. Even in the aftermath of electoral defeat, the prophet in Wilson continued to preach his own gospel, condemning those who would not see the world in his own light. He continued to pursue the goals of the Fourteen Points even though Roosevelt had rejected them outright insofar as Republican co-operation was concerned. He declared, : "Our allies and our enemies and Mr. Wilson himself should all understand that Mr. Wilson has no authority to speak for the American people at this time. His leadership has just been enthusiastically repudiated by them."

Had Wilson been more of a politician and less of a preacher and Roosevelt more of a statesman and less of a politician, the prophetic vision of world peace might have been salvaged. Neither leader was being a shrewd politician or statesman in proceeding with less than a clear majority of voters supporting the peace plan, and it failed because of that tactical error.

As a political blunder of the first order, Wilson appointed to the Paris Peace Conference—himself, Colonel House, Secretary of State Lansing, General Tasker H. Bliss, and a lone Republican diplomat Henry White. The work of the conference was doomed to failure in Washington before the President and his group ever left for Paris. There were even questions raised about the legality of a sitting President leaving the country during his term of office, since no one had ever done so before. That aside, the country was led to have serious doubts about what secret decisions were to be made in the "smoke-filled rooms in Paris."

In Paris Wilson was able to use the considerable moral power of the United States, as well as that of his own, to force the adoption of statesman-like terms ending the war as well as the incorporation of the League of Nations in the treaty itself. In theory it was to be universal and permanent, an arrangement to forestall wars in the future. It was projected to include all states which applied. In the Assembly, the congress of the world, each state would have one vote, but in the Council the "Big Five" world powers each had a permanent seat and smaller states rotated after election of the Assembly. The heart of the document was contained in Article Ten, by which the members pledged to respect and mutually preserve the independence of all members against aggression. This process of collective security was obviously the same basis upon which the United Nations was organized in 1945.

Before leaving Paris to return home for a few days to sign bills passed in his absence, President Wilson cabled the chairmen of the respective foreign affairs committees of both House and Senate, asking them to withhold judgment until he might have a chance to explain the treaty. He did just that, in private conversations with key members of Congress. Lodge would have none of it, and on March 4 he introduced in the Senate his "Round Robin," rejecting the treaty and any form of the League which it might contain. When the Democrats protested, Lodge read into the record the names of thirty-seven Republican senators and senators-elect who had signed the document, signaling that it had no chance of approval by the Senate since there was not a two-thirds vote for it. Wilson struck back in anger: "When the treaty comes back for approval, gentlemen will find the Covenant not only in it, but so many threads of the treaty tied to the Covenant that you cannot dissect the Covenant from the treaty without destroying the whole . . . ."

Upon returning to Paris, Wilson found that the entire situation had changed; the long knives had come out, and it was every nation for itself. There was a general consensus that the Germans had to pay, which Wilson resisted. Even the Germans found new backbone, insisting that the new harsh demands upon them would surely lead to a new war in the future. Issues having absolutely nothing to do with the outbreak of the war were dragged in to satisfy one nation or another. Wilson fought a losing battle, and in the end the masters of Europe were too much for him; he was forced to sacrifice the spirit of the Fourteen Points to save his cherished League. He was out-negotiated, and he returned home a broken man, a prophet without honor in his own land or abroad.

Before Wilson landed in New York, Lodge had been at work plotting the defeat of the League and the treaty, because he believed it represented an objectionable internationalization of imperialism, that it promised more security than it could guarantee, and that it surrendered the Republican Party's perceived ascendancy in the field of foreign relations. Even so, Lodge was a moderate compared to some senators, such as William E. Borah, who led a bloc of about a dozen senators who were absolutely opposed to the League in any manner, shape, or form. Instead, Lodge and the Republican center sought to "improve" the League concept by adding amendments, which they knew or understood would be rejected by Wilson or by the European powers.

The Lodge strategy was key because the Republican majority in the Senate was razor thin, 49 Republicans to 47 Democrats, so the effort to draw in as many votes against for whatever reason was crucial. Lodge was not an isolationist, nor was he opposed to any form of international cooperation. His motivation was hostility to Wilson for partisan reasons. Moderate Republican and "irreconcilable" votes were enough to kill the League, but Lodge was also interested in wresting control of foreign policy from Democratic hands and neutralizing the leadership of Wilson. To do so he launched a massive propaganda campaign financed by Andrew Carnegie and Henry C. Frick. In the first round they obtained and published a draft of the treaty. Nothing was contained therein which had not already been leaked, but the damage was done by insinuating that it contained something sinister. With public doubts raised, Wilson was never able to overcome them. The ace up his sleeve was that the League was *in* the treaty, and to reject that would leave the whole question of ending the war unresolved.

What followed was an all-out effort to change the minds and hearts of the American voters. As Wilson took his show on the road, stopping at the least likely places to talk to all who would listen, a Republican "truth squad" followed, eager to undo his conversions. That strenuous effort took its toll on the aging President and caught up with him at Pueblo, Colorado. There at the county fair Wilson spoke passionately about the treaty and the League: "If the nations do not embrace this last effort to prevent the wars of the past, I can predict with absolutely certainty that this nation will in another generation be tried again in another conflict even greater." Prophetic words, indeed. The exhausted President was rushed back to Washington and later suffered a stroke. The nation was without a chief executive, and the League was without its chief architect and spokesman.

The sick Wilson lay confined to bed for weeks, and the young, second Mrs. Wilson effectively exercised the powers of the his office by selecting those who were admitted to the bedroom. When Lodge and a few senators came to call and to check on Wilson's consciousness, upon leaving Lodge said, "We are praying for you, Mr. President." "Which way, Senator?" dryly retorted Wilson. He stuck to his guns and refused any compromise on the League, and so did Lodge. So the treaty went down to defeat, 49 in favor and 35 against. Wilson expected his party to make the League the central issue in the 1920 election. A week before that election, he suggested that every candidate for any office be required publicly to answer the question, "Shall we, or shall we not, redeem the great moral obligation of the United States?" Both parties declined to debate the issue. Cox, the Democratic candidate, quietly supported the League, but he declined to fight for it, and the League was forgotten. Europe did organized the League, and it functioned for a few years until it was challenged and failed to meet the test of effectiveness. Without the moral power of the nation and the leader which had launched it, it had no chance of success.

In due course, the United States made a separate treaty of peace with Germany, without the League articles. Then it withdrew from European, if not all, possible foreign involvements. The nation was sick of war and soured on the taste of idealism, and it watched as Hitler, Mussolini, and Stalin and other dictators came to power and threatened the peace of the world. It did nothing to contain them, either in its own right or in concert with other nations. It wanted a breather from high moral principles, and it let out its collective corset and lived a little. Wilson soon died after leaving office and was laid to rest in the impressive, new National Cathedral, a great prophet and statesman, but a failed political leader. There has never been another President like him since, and based on that experience there is not likely to be another. Higher, post-graduate education in diplomacy and world affairs has since seen as something of a *de facto* disqualification for the office of President.

Was it possible for the United States to have avoided involvement in the war without endangering its vital national interests and security? Was it the fault of Wilson or Lodge, or both, that the League of nations failed? Does not party politics bear great blame for seeking to resolve such an issue in the cockpit of a presidential campaign? Does the American public also bear some blame for allowing themselves to be bamboozled by both parties over such a critical question? Even in a democracy, is it fair or reasonable to expect ordinary citizens to exercise sound judgment under such circumstances? Did not American politicians mortgage the security of the United States, if not of the entire world, in the foolish and short-sighted attempt to gain partisan advantage from the League question? Do American presidents have the right or reasonable expectation that the nation will follow their leadership in foreign affairs for the period following their election so long as their leadership remains consistent with the principles on which they were elected? Was this not an ideal time to seek a bi-partisan solution to a question which transcended the views and interests of either party? Which vital interests of the United States were served in the rejection of the League? Where were the learned experts in foreign policy to warn the public of the great and tragic mistake they were about to make? To whom shall be sent the un-payable bill for this mistake in national judgment? Those who made the supreme sacrifice deserve answers to these questions.

In Flanders field the poppies blow
Between the crosses, row on row,
That marks our place, and in the sky,
The larks, still singing, fly
Scarce heard among the guns below.

Take up our quarrel with the foe!
To you from failing hands we throw
The torch; be yours to hold on high,
If ye break faith with us who die
We shall not sleep, though poppies grow
In Flanders field.

—John McCrea, 1915

CHAPTER 4

AMERICAN ENTRY INTO WORLD WAR II

The Republican brand of foreign policy of the pre-and post-Depression era was cautious and conservative, which matched exactly the mood of the country. Americans cared little and thought less about international problem of the period. They were "idealized out" by being stretched by Wilson's high-mindedness, and they wished to indulge themselves by having fun and attending to business. In the process they allowed threats to world peace to grow to gigantic size, secure in false hope that by willing it so, the dangers would pass America by. They did not.

The driving force of the period and its foreign policy issues were the desire to save the expenses of large armaments, so it became settled policy for Harding, Coolidge, and Hoover to cut back on the size of the army and to negotiate the proportionate reduction of the active-duty, battle-line ships of the navy. The fact that almost all nations eventually cheated on their allotted quotas was an open secret, which in turn led to an arms race and preparation for conflict before it became imminent. The United States allowed itself to remain totally unprepared for the conflict which was so clearly in the process by 1935. Politicians of both parties share in the responsibility of their failure to protect the national vital interests.

President Franklin Roosevelt was superbly qualified to lead the nation during his time in office. Elected by a landslide which constituted a clear mandate, and adored by a public which viewed him as a political messiah, he was both politician and statesman, and in the field of foreign policy he often displayed the same craftiness by which earned his reputation in domestic affairs. In dealing with other nations, even those with which the United States was nominally allied, he could be condescending and determined to have his way—yet he was generally liked by world leaders. He trusted his own judgment to such an extent that at times he made errors regarding national interests. To say the least, he was a charismatic and complicated leader, and he left his long shadow upon American foreign policy and on the world when he died in 1945.

World War II, that which was so prophetically foretold by President Wilson, came in 1939 on the Eastern Front with the unprovoked attack upon Poland. Within hours after the exchange of declarations of war, President Roosevelt declared, "This nation remains a neutral nation, but I cannot ask that every American remain in thought as well." Included in his declaration was also a pledge to attempt to keep the United States out of the conflict. A master communicator as well as master politician, by doing so he escaped repeating the mistakes which Wilson had made 30 years earlier. He began carefully to build a consensus at the very beginning of the conflict, and in their hearts most Americans knew that sooner or later the United States would become involved.

The German war machine rolled over the weak but stubborn resistance mounted by the Poles, but it soon became evident that this new kind of warfare would be different. It would consist of lightning strikes, the so-called *blitzkrieg* as advocated by General Erwin Rommel and based on the tactics employed by Stonewall Jackson in the American Civil War. Traditional defense against such tactics were useless, and there was not much time to train a new army and employ counter-tactics, so Roosevelt's foreign policy was designed to buy time. Two weeks after the war began he asked Congress to revise the neutrality laws to meet the new war-time conditions in Europe. The leaders of Congress privately informed Roosevelt that his wishes could not be made law and that he would have to accept a compromise. He willingly went along because he had no alternative.

After several weeks of spirited debate, Congress passed the Fourth Neutrality Act, along strict party lines. When the President signed the bill on November 4, 1939, American neutrality during wartime was radically altered. The new law raised an interesting constitutional question in that Congress reserved for itself the creation of foreign policy by "finding" a state of war existed in case the President was derelict in doing so. Other provisions of the act relaxed the ban on loans to belligerents and forbade American ships to enter a war zone regardless of cargo or final destination. Perhaps most important of all, the new act allowed American firms to sell munitions to belligerents on a "cash and carry" basis. The old, traditional law of neutrality in its application had favored Germany in World War I; in World War II, it would favor Britain and her allies—precisely the purpose of the President. The act obviously recalled the efforts of Wilson and the Grey-House Memorandum which had sought to end World War I.

Just as the Allies had been in World War I when they were not interested in a negotiated peace, so both sides settled down into what was called at the time the "phony war," war which was not a war, but an armed truce, each side waiting for the other to take the initiative. The prevailing view or hope in America was that the superior economic and sea power of the British and French would ultimately topple Hitler, thereby saving American involvement in another conflict. Attempting to use its historic advantage on the high seas, Britain imposed a strict blockade against Germany without regard to the rights of neutrals. Hitler, in turn, imposed a submarine blockade against Britain, thereby guaranteeing eventual conflict with America. In actual practice, Roosevelt pressed the Germans hard for their violations of American rights while looking to the other way against British violations. It was a policy of "un-neutral neutrality," and Hitler lost to time in pointing out the actual practice of America violated its own definition of international law. The worst case the United States had against Britain was the censoring of mail bound for Germany. The United States was again in the cross-fire and inching into war.

The *blitzkrieg* and subsequent stalemate was relieved by the conflict between little Finland and the Soviet Union which broke out in the winter of 1939-1940. Threatened for their very existence, the brave Finns appealed to the American President for help, but the only help forthcoming was the offer to mediate the conflict. Encouraged by the American inactivity, the Russian army rolled into Finland. American public opinion was outraged, having a special fondness for the plucky little nation, the only one which had paid its debts after World War I. The best the American government could do was to grant a moratorium and extend new loans to Finland, restricting the proceeds to peaceful purposes. Shaming the "talking heads" of the day, the Finns held off the combined might of the Soviet army for several months before being forced to cede a strip of land on the Russian border and accept the forced re-location of about a fourth of the Finnish population. American public opinion of Russia was so soured at the end of the Winter War that war against the Soviet Union *and* Germany was a distinct possibility.

Events on another part of the chessboard of Europe occupied the world's attention in 1940. A new round of *blitzkrieg* was launched against Belgium, Holland, and into France, with another spearhead into the Scandinavian neighbors of Denmark and Norway. They all resisted heroically, but they were all conquered and their governments forced to flee in exile to Britain. In June, with all the world seeming to crumble, Mussolini, the Italian dictator, jumped into the war on the side of Germany in order to collect some of the spoils. Sorely pressed, the British army in France struggled to escape total defeat at Dunkirk, and the French Premier, Paul Raynaud, phoned Roosevelt earnestly to beg for help: "Can you stretch your hand across the ocean to help us and save civilization?" On June 5, Roosevelt responded by lifting the embargo on arms sales by offering arms and ammunition left over from World War I. America was taking another step towards war.

Roosevelt's most recent policy change marked a turning point in American foreign policy. Utilizing the forum of a graduation speech at the University of Virginia, he declared that because of the recent turn of events in Europe, America was re-defining its role to become a "non-belligerent." That meant the United States was prepared to offer every assistance short of war to the Allies. To the American people he announced his clear intent: "In our American unity, we will pursue two obvious courses; we shall extend to the opponents of force the material resources of this nation, and at the same time we will harness and speed up the use of those resources in order that we ourselves in the Americas may have equipment and training equal to the task of any emergency and every defense." In other words, America would pray for peace but prepare for war. Those young Americans who could not wait for a chance to fight Hitler rushed across the Atlantic and joined Britain's military. Shortly afterward, France fell "like a drowning man." Feeling the pain of the French distress, Roosevelt reminded the French Premier that "only Congress could make such commitments" as France was desperately asking for.

On June 22, in the identical rail car in which Germany had been forced to surrender in World War I, Hitler extracted his vengeance and danced his little victory dance while the tables were turned and France suffered the humiliation of defeat. Only by total surrender was a remnant of France under Marshal Petain, a hero of World War I, able to survive. Petain could promise his countrymen nothing less than "blood, sweat, and tears." In the United States the fall of France profoundly shocked public opinion. Some wanted to fix the blame on American leaders for allowing that to happen. Others wanted America to embark on a crash course of preparedness before the United Stated suffered a similar fate. Still others wanted an outright and immediate declaration of war against Germany.

A presidential election was under way in 1940, but the Republican candidate, Wendell Willkie, refused to capitalize on the circumstances and the divisions in public opinion regarding the war in Europe. William Allen White, and old friend of the President, observed in a letter to Roosevelt, "Let me warn you that maybe you will not be able to lead the American people unless you catch up with them. They are going too fast." In summary, the election of 1940 was a case of foreign policy being remarkably free of party politics. To whatever degree there were divisions in American public opinion on how rapidly and openly the United States should respond to the threat to world domination posed by the Axis Powers, those divisions did not follow party lines. It is fair to say that an overwhelming percentage of the American people were ready to follow their president into the conflict, if that were deemed necessary, and were waiting for him to call them to action. Realizing that public opinion had reached a critical juncture, Roosevelt altered course and began openly and actively to favor the Allied cause. The steps by which the United States entered World War II may be studied as something of a model of foreign policy being responsibly developed and timed.

First, the President froze all economic assets of the Axis powers. Spain, which had allied herself with Hitler as a non-belligerent, suffered the same fate. Calculating what could happen if Germany acquired the fleets of Britain and France, Roosevelt pressured Congress to appropriate funds to build a two-ocean navy, and the nation went on a virtual war footing while the army was still training with broom sticks for guns and rapidly transforming recruits into a fighting organization. In what perhaps turned out to be most important of all, Roosevelt responded to a letter from Albert Einstein regarding the theoretical possibility of developing an atomic super bomb by launching the Manhattan Project, which produced the first atomic weapons before the end of the war.

The most serious challenge to the bi-partisan push for preparedness was the matter of raising an army of the size needed, and that required the use of a draft. When Roosevelt requested such authorization, the isolationists in both parties, but not the leaders of either party, screamed in protest. Senator Gerald Nye spoke for those extremists: "The only emergency in this country is the one conjured up by those who want to send our boys to Europe and Asia." After spirited debate, the first peace-time draft squeaked by, and the process was begun of building an army to match the navy which was already in process of being built. Here was an example of bi-partisan co-operation in establishing a foreign policy based on the long-term prospects which best protected and promoted national interests, and it can serve as a model in the future.

While the nation and the President was preoccupied with the German problem, on the other side of the world Japan was flexing its military muscle and threatening to cause trouble for America in the Far East. Japan's internal structure shifted from a civilian government to one dominated by military and naval leaders, a move Japan justified by the economic squeeze being placed by the Allies and the United States. It must be said that American policy towards Japan had been wary since the early 1930's, as it sought to bring China under its domination and showed clear signs of seeking even more aggressive goals. As it turned out, it was a race in 1941 to see in which theater an incident would take place to bring the United States into the conflict. America was profoundly disturbed in 1941 when Japan took advantage of French inability to defend its interests and territory by military occupation of Indo-China (Vietnam).

European stability was again threatened by the German *blitzkrieg* in 1940-41, and Japan took further advantage of the opportunity by moving against the territory and interests of the powers of Europe. That alarmed some very influential Americans, including members of the powerful Committee to Defend America by Aiding the Allies. However enlightened the committee and one of its leaders, William Allen White, such a pressure group operating in the field of foreign policy constituted a potential threat to presidential responsibility to conduct foreign policy. It sought to keep America out of the war by being prepared and by openly assisting the Allies, and it served as an effective counter-weight to isolationism. Nevertheless, such citizen groups should always be mindful that they tread closely upon presidential prerogatives. Roosevelt was effective in using such groups to his own advantage, but less gifted presidents have been overly influenced or impeded by them.

One of the most critical needs of the British in 1940 was more destroyers to guards conveys carrying war material to the European theater—and the American navy had a surplus of such vessels left over from World War I. Supply and demand were brought together in July, 1940, when the President, on his own authority as Commander-in-Chief as well as the constitutional authority to conduct foreign relations, swapped fifty over-age ships for 99-year leases for American bases in British possessions in the Atlantic and the Caribbean. Strictly speaking, the President probably exceeded his constitutional authority, but because the correct kind of suit was never filed, the Supreme Court never spoke to the issue. The Chicago *Tribune* fumed, "The sale of the Navy's ships to a nation at war would be an act of war. If we want to get into the war, the destroyers offer as good a way as any of accomplishing the purpose." Undeterred, the President confirmed the deal on September 2, and as an outright gift Prime Minister Churchill also gave the United States bases in Bermuda and Newfoundland. Churchill also exceeded his authority under British law, but that was a matter for another nation to untangle. The deal made the United States almost—but not quite—a legal ally of Britain. The President justified his action to Congress as "an epochal and far-reaching preparation for common defense in the face of grave danger." Although most Americans thought the deal a good one, to have the American President to justify stretching his constitutional authority beyond the limits was a novel constitutional theory. The minority press thundered its condemnation. The *St. Louis Post-Dispatch* declared, "Dictator Roosevelt Commits an Act of War!" and America First leaders covered the nation with tracts expressing similar views. Believing that Hitler and his Axis allies posed no immediate threat to American interests or security, they demanded that American foreign policy be based upon and serve "America First." Despite such minority views, Roosevelt persisted in his policies. Reading the temperature of the public, he was certain of his base of support.

Such a critical division of American opinion on such a crucial issue is an excellent illustration of the thesis of this little volume. Once a settled foreign policy involving potential war has been established with broad popular support, continued carping exposes the nation to mortal danger. There are more responsible ways for political action groups to focus the attention of the public to their grievances and to change American foreign policy. The statement issued by America First that "American Democracy can be preserved only by keeping out of the European war" was not only wrong, it was also dangerous. It is not desirable or necessary for American foreign policy always to be decided at the ballot box. In those cases when debate cannot take place outside of national crisis, there are other and more safe means of shaping foreign policy. An American citizen who allows himself to be so misled under such circumstances is also guilty of contributing to the chaos in foreign policy. Just so, a political leader who seeks to take advantage of the emotional aspects in national crisis in order to change foreign policy carries a heavy burden to justify his conduct.

The burning question in the presidential election of 1940 was who, if anyone, was more qualified to replace Franklin Roosevelt as President? That was almost tantamount to stating that Roosevelt was indispensable. Even so, he defied tradition, stood for a third term, and won. That was partly due to the fact that the "international" wing of the Republican Party outflanked the "isolationist" wing, and offered only token opposition. In fact, the Republican platform in 1940 did not differ from the Democratic one in any significant degree regarding foreign policy. In the heat of the campaign, when the Republican old guard urged Willkie to step up the attack on Roosevelt's handling of foreign affairs (using foreign policy to secure domestic ends), Roosevelt returned the favor by proclaiming, "I have said this before, but I shall say it again and again . . . . Your boys are not going to be sent into any foreign war." Even if Roosevelt in his heart knew that such a pledge could not be honored, he also knew how to play political hardball when circumstances demanded.

With the election won, Roosevelt soon moved more aggressively to support the Allied cause. In his 1941 Annual Message to Congress he asked for passage of the Lend-Lease Act, whereby American war material would be sent to the Allies on credit because they were fighting war to preserve "four essential freedoms—of speech, of worship, from war, and from fear,—thereby internationalizing those freedoms guaranteed by the American Constitution. Again, this was interesting constitutional law but questionable legal grounds for pursuing foreign policy. Senator Robert Taft of Ohio carried the isolationist opposition to the bill because it would give "the President power to carry on a kind of undeclared war all over the world, in which America would do everything except actually put soldiers in the front-line trenches where the fighting is." However one might disagree with the *policy* Senator Taft was resisting, one has difficulty resisting his logic. Ultimately, the Lend-Lease Act passed in the House by a vote of 260 to 165, and in the Senate, 60 to 31. The resulting law entitled, "An Act to Promote the Defense of the United States," authorized the President to "sell, lease, or lend under such terms as he thought proper, arms, ammunition, food, and other defense articles to any country whose defense he deemed vital to the defense of the United States." The Act also forbade the navy from convoying to their destination the lend-lease articles, but by conceding that small point to isolationist sentiment the President was again taking the nation closer to a war footing and making it *de facto* an ally of the Allies.

With the remarkable candor with which he was known, the American Chief of Naval Operations, Admiral Ernest J. King, wrote privately to the fleet commanders, "The question as to our entry into the war now seems to be *when,* and not *whether.*" Naval commanders do not always write political observations in such succinct language, and perhaps it is a practice which should be encouraged by their political superiors. What followed was an undeclared war in the Atlantic, German submarines not being overly fastidious in selecting their targets, and American ships shooting back when attacked. From and after June, 1941, the United States was at war with German submarines, and Navy personnel earned combat ribbons to prove it.

A special relationship developed during the months leading up to American entry into the war between the American President and the British Prime Minister, and that relationship deeply influenced American foreign policy, both during the war and in planning the post-war peace. More than just a personal friendship between two similar men, it was a symbiotic pairing between cultural twins. They instinctively liked and admired each other, and that friendship spilled over into policies of both governments. Roosevelt often said, "I have just got to see Churchill myself, in order to explain things to him." They first met at sea, off the coast of Newfoundland, and in four days of the closest kind of give and take they planned the conduct of the war, one in which the United States was not yet a party. Regarding the growing menace from Japan, Churchill urged Roosevelt to promise to use American naval power to block Japanese expansion into Southeast Asia, but Roosevelt demurred on grounds that he could not commit American forces without the consent of Congress. On matters of even greater import, however, the American President was not so reticent. Desiring boldly to define war aims, Roosevelt and Churchill readily agreed on what was to be called the Atlantic Charter: (1) neither country sought territorial aggrandizement; (2) both disclaimed any territorial adjustments; (3) both recognized the right of all people to self-government; (4) without unsettling trade agreements, both countries declared in favor of free trade; (5) both pledged international co-operation in advancing labor standards; (6) both declared in favor of freedom from want and fear; (7) both firmly re-stated the principle of freedom of the seas; and (8) both promised to support a new system to guarantee mutual security and disarmament. In other words, Woodrow Wilson must have smiled in his grave that the League of Nations would have a second birth.

It is well to keep in mind what was *not* made as a commitment in the Atlantic Charter. The very act of making such an agreement with a belligerent made the United States *de facto* a co-belligerent. The national newspaper of record, the New York *Times* editorialized, "President Roosevelt is retracing one by one all of the steps taken by President Wilson—steps which the American people later and in the light of calm reflection and sober judgment overwhelmingly stamped as mistakes." The President defended himself by declaring that he had made no new promises, and that he believed that a shooting war involving the United States was more likely in Asia than in Europe. But in the last analysis, the President was correct. In the midst of the fallout from the Atlantic Charter debate, events in far-off Iran seriously outweighed concerns of American merchant vessels and providing convoying to insure that American goods reached Britain and Russia. Germany retaliated on October 16 by sinking the USS *Kearny* off Iceland with the loss of many lives. Four days later the USS *Rueben James* met a similar fate. Some wag at the time was quoted as saying, "You cannot shoot your way a little bit into a war any more than you can get a woman a little pregnant. He also declared that he was willing to stand by his policy and be judged by history.

In the midst of the fallout from the Atlantic Charter debate, events in far-off Iran seriously strained relations between the two leaders and further inflamed disagreements about the underlying foundations of the Charter. The issue of Iran came after Britain and Russia, frustrated by the inability or unwillingness of the Shah to reform his regime, invaded Iran to keep open the flow of lend-lease supplies to Russia. Rather than embarrass itself, or its British and quasi-*de-facto* allies, the United States took no action. The Iranian Ambassador protested to sober, gentlemanly Secretary of State Cordell Hull the failure of the United States "to carry out its own preachments of the eight principles underlying peaceful and free nations."

Internationalists and isolationists continued to snipe at each other, while the U. S. Navy was soon in a shooting war in the Atlantic. On the night of September 4, the USS *Greer* shadowed a German submarine for several hours, constantly reporting its position to the British fleet. When the U-boat skipper decided to fight back and fired two torpedoes at the *Greer*, the President went on national radio to denounce the attack as "piracy, legally and morally," despite the undeniable fact that the American destroyer started it all in the first place. In retaliation, the President announced that thereafter, American planes and ships would convoy British and American vessels carrying goods to Britain. To make it even more clear, the President gave the Navy orders to "shoot on sight" any German vessels it might encounter. Again, Admiral King, the same crusty Chief of Naval Operations declared, "So far as the Atlantic is concerned, we are all but, if not actually in it." In addition to being in command of the U. S. Navy, Admiral King demonstrated a command of the English language. The Navy understood its orders and the circumstances, and it flawlessly performed.

Roosevelt's next step into war came in asking Congress to revise the neutrality acts to permit the arming of American merchant vessels and providing convoying to insure that American goods reached Britain and Russia. Germany retaliated on October 16 by sinking the USS *Kearny* off Iceland with the loss Britain and Russia. Germany retaliated on October 16 by sinking the USS *Kearny* off Iceland with the loss of eleven American sailors. Four days later the USS *Rueben James* met a similar fate. Some wag at the time was quoted as saying, "You cannot shoot your way a little bit into a war any more than you can float a little bit over Niagara Falls."

The American march towards war now shifted to the Pacific.

A great deal of foolish non-sense, if not deliberate falsehood, has been spent on whether or not President Roosevelt "lied us" into the war, or rather, so staked out the Pacific fleet as to invite an attack by Japan, thus securing a national consensus to enter the war. It *is* a fact that American code-breakers had broken the Japanese *diplomatic* codes (Operation Magic) prior to Pearl Harbor. By reading the Japan diplomatic mail the American leadership knew that *something* was about to happen on or about the first week of December. Specifically *what* was being planned *where* by the Japanese was not known. Intelligence personnel thought that Japan was preparing to make the long-awaited thrust into Southeast Asia—which it did in fact do, simultaneous with the attack on Pearl Harbor. American code-breakers did *not* break the Japanese naval codes, but when important units of the Japanese navy went to radio silence a week before, it should have suggested that an important attack was likely. For whatever reason, no one sounded the alarm for an attack on Hawaii. The attack on Pearl Harbor was, therefore a surprise and a tactical success but a strategic blunder, which finally aroused and united the American people.

There followed for the next four years a world conflict unprecedented in scope and scale, involving a larger proportion of the world's population, with a casualty toll greater than ever before in history. Virtually the whole world was ultimately engaged in war between Germany, Italy, and Japan, on the one hand, and Britain, the United States, Russia, and the Allies on the other. Finally, in 1945, the Allies were finally able to force Germany and then Japan to capitulate.

Let us now shift to a summary of the planning the Grand Coalition's conduct of the war and the peace which was to follow. Unfortunately, that turned out to be more difficult and less successful than actually winning the war itself.

Immediately after Pearl Harbor, Churchill flew to Washington with a large contingent of senior military leaders to plan Allied strategy. During December to January, 1942, the British slowly convinced the Americans to concentrate first on the enemy in Europe, because Germany controlled the larger population pool and war resources, representing a greater threat. That meant that fewer resources would be allocated to the Pacific, and that aid to the Nationalist Chinese would be given only the lowest priority because that area of combat was remote from Allied bases of power. In Washington on New Year's Day, 1942, the United States, the United Kingdom, Russia, and representatives of twenty-three other nations already at war with the Axis pledged to uphold the principles of the Atlantic Charter, not to sign a separate peace, and to commit themselves to forming the United Nations at the end. Before the ink was dry on these promises, Churchill and Roosevelt were confronted by Russian demands for territorial demands in Eastern Europe which violated the spirit if not the letter of these ideals. The best that Roosevelt and Churchill would do was to postpone consideration of these issues until later, at the cost of promising Russia a "Second Front," and landing in Europe, in 1942.

Given American determination to relieve the pressure on the Russians, but British conviction that a landing in Europe in 1942 could not be mounted, another Allied war strategy session took place at Hyde Park in June. The result was the North African campaign, launched in November, 1942, as a substitute to a landing in Europe. Stalin was not satisfied with the substitution, but he accepted it because he had no alternative. Green American troops were bloodied when they first confronted Marshal Erwin Rommel's Afrika Corps, but the coalition of British, American, and Free

French forces slowly turned the tide, kept the Suez Canal open for the duration of the war, and made possible the Casablanca Conference in January, 1943, at which the Allies announced the determination to fight on until the "unconditional surrender" of all the Axis Powers. That policy was doggedly advocated by Roosevelt, and it reflected his understanding of all that had gone wrong at the end of World War I and his determination to avoid a repetition. At Casablanca the British had pushed for the next campaign in Europe to be through Greece and the Balkans, suspecting Russian intentions in the area post-war. That idea was shelved in favor of the campaign in Sicily and Italy, Britain's second choice, and Stalin claimed breach of promise. Back in the United States the leadership of the Republican Party at a conference on Mackinac Island pledged their co-operation in establishing a mutual-defense organization at the end of the war. That was followed in the fall by lop-sided votes of 360 to 29 in the House and 85 to 5 in the Senate for the Fulbright-Connally Resolution pledging support for the concept of a post-war organization "with power to prevent aggression and preserve the peace of the world." It seemed that the United Nations would have an easy birth in the vortex of American politics.

The next conference of the Allies was in Quebec, Canada, in August, 1943, where the cross-channel invasion was planned along with acceptance of Italy into the alliance after Mussolini was captured and killed. At the same time, with the heavy lifting having been done to plan the end of the war in Europe, plans were made to shift the focus to the Pacific, where American forces had been slowly mopping up the numerous islands the Japanese had previously overrun. As a follow-on, Stalin promised to join the war against Japan as soon as Germany surrendered.

Sensing that agreements with long-range consequences were being made without the personal participation of Stalin, Roosevelt urged a meeting of himself, Churchill, and Stalin in the fall of 1943. Perhaps revealing too much diplomatic capacity on his part, Roosevelt wrote to the British Prime Minister: "I tell you, that I think I can personally handle Stalin better than either your Foreign Office or my State Department." Stalin stubbornly refused to leave his own "comfort zone," so the meeting was held in Teheran, Iran. Roosevelt was in declining health, but he made the arduous trip, and for five days he was exposed to Stalin's best efforts to drive a wedge between the British and Americans. The results were an iron promise of a cross-channel invasion in 1944, coupled with the solemn promise of Russia to help in the defeat of Japan following German surrender. Roosevelt left Teheran optimistic about Russian co-operation in the post-war world. Apparently, most Americans agreed with him at this time, for in November, 1944, he coasted to a fourth-term victory against Thomas E. Dewey. Again, there was little difference between the foreign policy platforms of the two parties, but because he was disturbed by the mere appearance of the division which had unhorsed Wilson, he lashed out, "The power which this Nation has attained—the political, the economic, the military, and above all the moral power—has brought to us the responsibility, and with it the opportunity, for leadership in the community of Nations. In our own best interest, and in name of peace and humanity, this Nation cannot, must not, and will not shrink that responsibility."

Proceeding on that new mandate, Roosevelt administration sponsored conferences at Breton Woods and Dumbarton Oaks, at which were created the International Monetary Fund to stabilize post-war the world currencies and the International Bank for Reconstruction and Finance, to provide capital to devastated areas needing reconstruction. While these actions represented progress, the kind of co-operation and the attitude exhibited by Russia began to signal rough weather ahead. The concerns were taken to the next conference at Yalta in February, 1945. There Roosevelt and Churchill agreed to new boundaries for Poland and thought they secured the framework by which the Poles themselves would decide the shape of their own government. In return, they secured the promise of prompt Russian entry into the war against Japan, then thought to be indispensable. As it turned out, the atomic bomb made Russian participation superfluous, and Russian occupation of Poland and Eastern Europe made any Russians promises affecting the area capable of being ignored. It was on the basis of these two critical developments that political opposition was first made against the policies agreed to at Yalta and to the future of American relations with the Soviet Union. The brilliant successes of leadership in foreign policy and in the strategy of the war was reversed by the removal of that leadership.

Too soon, as the shooting was winding down, the President who had led the nation to victory himself became a victim of it. A tired and obviously sick man returned from the Yalta Conference, which was the first look at the problem of the post-war world. Shortly thereafter, the Commander-in-Chief became the Sacrifice-in-Chief. The poetry and mood of the nation was the riderless horse, boots reversed in the stirrups, and a flag-draped coffin pulled by a matched gray team, solemnly bearing the hero to his final resting place overlooking the Hudson at Hyde Park. The President had become a war casualty as surely as if he had been slain on the battlefield, and he was accorded a war hero's final salute.

Was American involvement in World War II a war of "convenience" or of necessity? Was it necessary to suffer the death of over 3,000 American service personnel on that fateful December Sunday to accomplish what a masterful communicator had been unable previously to do? In what was the greatest of all world wars in which the Allies came so close time and time again to losing, was the combined costs of several million dead finally redeemed by arrangements to insure that such a conflict never again plagued mankind? Ask the survivors of Auschwitz and Buchenwald if the results were worth the costs. Ask the boys from the local company of the 29th Division from the little town of Bedford, Virginia, if it was all worth the sacrifice of two-thirds of their members on Omaha Beach. Ask the millions of Russian widows and war veterans if they have ample cause to remember that war, even if their nation sought to impose Communism upon a tired world in the aftermath. Ask the Japanese civilians who survived Hiroshima and Nagasaki if the world is better or worse for their suffering?

When the guns and dying were finally finished, the nations of the world came together to give peace one last chance, a last-ditch opportunity under the shadow of a nuclear holocaust. In the face of such supreme sacrifice which had just been made on the altar of freedom, it would seem obscene for anyone thereafter to play politics with foreign policy. Owing the dead such a debt, perhaps grim humor is the only possible poetic way of expressing the hopes and temper of the post-war world.

"Sometime they'll give a war, and nobody will come."
Carl Sandburg, 1936

CHAPTER 5

THE VIETNAMESE CONFLICT: THE PROCESS OF ENTERING AND LEAVING A WAR

"They made a wasteland and called it peace."
—Tacitus

The American foreign policy tragedy called the Vietnamese Conflict began as an advisory function in an area involved in a civil war, having little to do with American national interests. It continued into the most deadly shooting war since the end of World War II. The war was never declared as such by Congress, yet it rivaled the Civil War as to total casualties. It bitterly divided the country when unity was an absolute necessity during the Cold War. It almost unhorsed a president in disgrace; and it precipitated an unprecedented constitutional crisis at the center of the American government. At its end, the United States left Southeast Asia under highly unusual circumstances, and it left a deep scar on the national pysche. Vietnam itself was left a political and environmental wasteland, far worse than it had been before the conflict began. And the soldiers of honor brought back from the chaos of Vietnam social and personal ills which still plague American society today. About the only thing which could have added more pathos to the tragedy was to have had a lone Highland piper to give a last salute in honor of those whose names are carved on their monument in Washington. Other than these unhappy facts, Vietnam was a part of the post-war struggle against Communist expansion, in which the United States learned some very bitter lessons about the limitations of its vast military power, about the dangers of taking a divided nation into an unpopular war, and about the problems of allowing foreign policy issues not of the first order to play a prominent role in domestic politics. The lessons are still fresh more than thirty years after the fact.

The conflict in Vietnam began long before World War II, back in the 19th century when France, after a long struggle, subdued the area, as well as Annam, Tonkin, Cochinchina, and Cambodia, all tied in a lose confederation. Despite native resistance, once French authority was established the urban Indochinese became thoroughly French, while the rural areas clung to their native languages and culture. The French culture in Indochina was only a thin veneer, however, and when peeled the area reverted to its cultural roots. About the time that the French were establishing control, a native leader, Ho Chi Minh, was born in Indochina of peasant ancestry. As soon as he could afford to do so, he left his native land for the next thirty years and became a Communist as a means of securing native independence. More about Ho later.

Indochina played no role in the fighting or the peace following World War I, but when Ho attempted to petition President Wilson for self-determination in the Treaty of Paris, he was ignored, thereby becoming a bitter enemy of the United States. Ho joined the French Communist Party and departed for Moscow, where he trained as an agent of world Communist expansion under Michael Borodin, the principal Soviet agent in in charge of the Far East.

French sovereignty, but not influence, in Indochina theoretically ended in 1932 when Bao Dai returned from his studies in Paris to ascend the throne under French control. The effort to establish a monarchy in Indochina actually backfired, giving Ho an additional justification for seeking to overthrow the French puppet regime in favor of self-government. When France was forced out of the war in 1940 and General Charles de Gaulle established a government in exile in London, the Japanese occupied French Indochina—but they left intact the French colonial administration. The reasons why Japan left French culture and administration in place while militarily occupying the area is a fascinating mystery and needs deeper historical analysis. The Japanese even secretly welcomed Ho to return to Indochina, where he promptly organized native resistance to French rule and Japanese occupation. Ho even co-operated with the American OSS during the war. Without a clearer examination it is hard to determine just who was running Indochina during the war, and which elements were supporting whom. Shortly after the Japanese attack on Pearl Harbor, General Nigugen Giap, an ally of Ho, formed the irregular Vietnamese army to secure by military action what Ho was seeking through politics—that is, to infiltrate the French colonial regime to prepare for independence after the country was cleared of the Japanese forces. Things in Indochina were indeed complicated, but they were to become even more so.

As World War II was winding down, the Japanese suddenly abolished the French colonial regime and replaced it with one of their own, but Bao Daui sought to outflank them by proclaiming independence for Indochina under Japanese protection. At the Pottsdam Conference, the United States agreed to have British forces disarm the Japanese south of the 16th parallel, Chinese Nationalist forces being assigned the task north of the line. What began as a simple military convenience soon took on a political life of it own. The United States obviously had no great interest in who controlled Indochina other than to favor self-determination whenever that became possible. It was generally assumed that it could take place in about a generation, but Ho jumped the gun by declaring independence as soon as the Japanese surrendered in August, 1945.

In a matter of a few days the British forces in Indochina handed over to the French control of the country, and Lieutenant-Colonel A. P. Dewey of the American OSS was the first American to die there in the native uprising. Early in 1946 China agreed to withdraw its troops from Vietnam north of the 16th parallel, and Vietnam was recognized as a "free state" within the French Union, with a referendum to decide if Tonkin, Annan, and Cochinchina were to be united with Vietnam. But something happened on the way to the referendum.

In May Ho Chi Minh went to Fountainbleu for negotiations, but Admiral Thierry, French High Commissioner for Vietnam, unilaterally declared that all previous agreements on the future of the area were null and void and proclaimed a separate government for Vietnam. That caused the negotiations to break down, but even so, Ho signed a *modus videndi* with the French and agreed to cease resistance. The renegade Admiral, a sort of French General Curtis LeMay, was dieing hard for the honor of colonial France. He shelled Haiphong, causing the Vietminh to withdraw from Hanoi and go underground to conduct a bloody guerrilla war against the French. The Admiral was finally removed by the French government, but not until a great deal of emotion had been unleashed and Vietnamese determination for independence was firmly established.

Until 1947 affairs in Vietnam had been outside the purview of most Americans, and they certainly lay outside the scope of official concern of the government of the United States. In that year, however, George Kennan of the State Department and admittedly an expert on all matters Russian, writing under the pen name "X", began to publicize the need if not the necessity of "containing" Communist expansion. His ideas were largely accepted uncritically. Before going further, as they pertained to Vietnam, it is appropriate to ask what vital interests of the United States were threatened. A great deal was justified under the rubric of the "domino effect" without any critical analysis as to how the area related to American interests or how the toppling of Vietnam might be related to American interests.

The Cold War was just heating up in 1947, and at the urging of President Truman Congress voted funds to curb Communist expansion into Greece and Turkey—without any convincing evidence being made public that those countries were in danger of subversion. That protection was later extended to *any* country which felt itself threatened to Communist expansion, a policy which came to be known as the Truman Doctrine. There may have been (and there probably was) intelligence to support that fear, but the concept was adopted without a general debate, and it became a settled and bi-partisan part of general American foreign policy, applicable to any and all parts of the world. The policy was especially focused on Western Europe through what came to be known as the Marshall Plan. In some sense, the United States invented or exaggerated the Communist threat outside of Europe and used it to justify massive foreign aid packages and pledges of military support, with the American taxpayers footing the bill.

There is no question that there was a real, definite threat from the expansion of Communism in many parts of the world where American interests were at risk, but the rubber, banana, of pineapple resources of Vietnam did not place it high on the list of such places. The justification for defending Vietnam was driven more by ideology than by objective economic or national security interests.

After Harry Truman narrowly defeated Thomas E. Dewey to win another term of his own as the President, Bao Dai and President Auriol of France signed an agreement early in 1949 making Vietnam an "associate state" within the French union. For the time being France retained control of foreign affairs and the finances of Vietnam. Simultaneously, the North Atlantic Treaty Organization (NATO) was being formed to defend Europe, and the Chinese Communist completed the take-over mainland China. At home, right-wing politicians looking for fodder to fight their domestic political battles went on a rampage to find the guilty parties who "gave China to the Communists." Russia exploded its first atomic bomb to underline the fact that matters were not going well for the United States on the world scene, and there was much political hay to be made from that fact.

On January 14, 1950, Ho declared that the Democratic Republic of Vietnam was the only and legitimate government, as it was *de facto* the regime in control. Ho immediately recognized the Soviet Union and China and soon thereafter added the Tito regime in Yugoslavia. Some American diplomatic officials rushed into print to declare that Ho was not Moscow's puppet, as they had previously insisted. In February the "containment faction" within the State Department won out, and the United States and Great Britain recognized the Bao Dai regime as that most likely to rise to power. The Chinese, now sharing a border with Vietnam, began to support Ho with arms and training. In June the North Korean attacked its neighbor to the south, erroneously assuming that the United States had drawn its defensive line to exclude South Korea. Truman responded, without a declaration of war, placing American troops under United Nations command. At the same time Truman approved the Congressional grant of $15 million to France for military operations in Vietnam. That last action was promptly rendered academic by the French defeat at Caobang, followed by the last-ditch appointment of General Jean de Lattre de Tassigny to stabilize Vietnam. France was running out of generals and options in Vietnam.

In 1951 Ho, having ridden the Communist train of convenience as far as it could take him, dissolved the Communist Party and in its place created the Workers Party. There were some important substantive changes made with this name change, strongly suggesting that Ho was open to some sort of understanding with the West. If so, those managing American foreign policy missed the signal. About the same time, General Douglas MacArthur was dismissed from command in Korea for what amounted to insubordination, and the right-wing of the Republican Party was whipped into a frenzy about the unhorsing of an American hero—whom they had hopes of electing President. Once on this slippery slope of policy, any American political leader who might have sought to reverse course in Vietnam would probably have been handed his head in the next election.

The next year General de Lattre had limited success in reining in the insurgent rebels, but he was take ill, returned home to seek medical attention, and France had no one of stature to replace him. The United States flexed its nuclear muscle by detonating its first hydrogen bomb, with sufficient notice to the world. General Giap in the interior of Vietnam was not impressed, but the Americans were, and they expected that such a weapon would make American power the law in international affairs. It did not happen, simply because the world did not believe that America would use the weapon except as a last resort to unprovoked attack.

1953 was a seminal year in the growing conflict in Vietnam. Joseph Stalin died on March 5 and was replaced by far less competent and less ruthless leaders with whom it might have been possible to reach an accommodation. France was mustering its courage to admit that it could not conquer the Vietnamese insurgents, and it raised no objections when Prince Sihanouk declared Cambodian independence. Ho again sent word that he was ready to negotiate, but no one in authority in Washington or London was interested in listening to what he had in mind. The possibility of a negotiated settlement of the future of Vietnam was carefully concealed from the American public.

Early 1954 the foreign ministers of the United States, Britain, France, and the Soviet Union met in Berlin and agreed to meet again in April on all issues involving Vietnam. What looked like the possible opening to peace then took a sudden turn with the fall of Dienbienphu, itself of no great importance, but its capture by rag-tag irregulars was a serious blow to French pride, a threat to perceived American security, and a tremendous boost to Ho's native army. The newly-elected President Eisenhower flatly rejected proposals to intervene with American military force, and Britain backed his decision.

The final loss of French control in Vietnam caused the fall of the government under Joseph Lanaiel, and the new Premier, Pierre Mendes-France, came to office with a promise to achieve a prompt cease fire and to set Vietnam free as soon as possible. On the ground in Vietnam Bao Dai selected Ngo Dinh Diem as Prime Minister, and it looked as if all parties were moving towards a peace accord. Without any public debate, the United States refused to accept without qualifications those agreements. Instead, it hastily cobbled together the Southeast Asia Treaty Organization (SEATO), including as members the United States, Britain, France, Australia, New Zealand, Pakistan, Thailand, and the Philippines. These countries in Asia were supposedly the targets of further expansion of Communism after it had overrun Vietnam. At the time there were persistent reports that arms were twisted to secure the treaty, but the documentary evidence, if any, of the charge has yet to be found. Suffice to ask under the circumstances, which American vital national interests were at stake in that part of the world? No European nation, not even the colonial power most immediately involved, seemed to have been concerned for anything other than loss of prestige.

General Lawton Collins was sent to Vietnam as Eisenhower's personal envoy, and he arrived with the pledge of $100 million in aid for Diem if the regime would stiffen its backbone to fight. It is amply documented that several American pressure groups played a role in establishing this policy, again none of it having to do with vital national interests. It would appear that there may have been a decision made at the highest policy councils of the American government to pick Vietnam as the stage on which to have it out with world Communist expansion. If so, America could not have picked a less comfortable and inaccessible theater in which to fight.

Why did American political leaders invite themselves and their nation into a war which apparently did not vitally concern them, without the unified support of the American or the native population, and which was apparently well on the way to settlement? The truth may be hidden in private manuscript collections and the public archives, but until we can know all the facts we are free to speculate. One guess is the interest which the American Catholic community shared with its Vietnamese counterparts, but that is not adequate to explain it in whole. Another possible reason was the over-concern for the Asiatic expansion of Communist China, but that possible reason is partially undercut by the fact that China was still enmeshed in its own cultural revolution. There is the gut feeling that there is more to be discovered regarding the reasons why American policy makers decided that Vietnam was worth fighting for.

In 1955 the United States began to slide the slope into what was essentially a civil war in Vietnam when it agreed to train the army and provide military advisers for field operations. During this period, the remaining French forces pulled back to the south while the Vietminh irregulars gathered in the north, thereby creating two separate regimes, foreign advisers propping up both sides. Given the evolving situation, Diem stiffened his resistance to the Geneva agreements, and he refused to participate in the nation-wide elections on July 16, taking his cue from the United States. Ho went off to Moscow to negotiate for Russian aid, having already received that promise from China. In the elections which only partially reflected national will, Diem defeated Bao Dai, thereby becoming chief of state of the Republic of Vietnam. In neighboring Cambodia, Prince Sihanhouk, the Prime Minister, announced his intention of following a purely neutral policy, against strong American pressure to continue supporting Vietnamese troops battling the Vietcong insurgents. Diem began a series of crack-downs on all those opposed to his regime, with the support of the United States. In Europe and the Middle East, the Soviets were crushing uprisings in Hungary and Poland; while Britain, France, and Israel launched the Suez War, which seriously strained the alliance against Communist expansion. Things were definitely not working out well for the United States, and a soul sickness began to appear in American public opinion, growing weary of fighting Communism.

The next blow to American prestige in Southeast Asia was the Soviet announcement that they favored a permanent division of Vietnam, with both parties being admitted to the United Nations. On a visit to the United States in 1957, Diem was warmly greeted by President Eisenhower over opposition from portions of the American public. The President announced that Hanoi had only recently raised about 40 companies of irregulars for service in the Mekong delta of South Vietnam. During the remainder of the year a reign of terror descended on South Vietnam during which over 400 minor officials were assassinated. Things seemed to be going from bad to worse in the area, and American prestige was at risk. American officials pressed the Vietnamese to become more aggressive in countering the insurgency.

In the fast-moving chain of events, it seemed that every day brought some new aspect or problem, and Washington was sorely tried in responding to them all. In Laos, Prince Souvanna Phouma dissolved his neutralist government, shortly thereafter succeeded by American-backed Phoui Sananikone amid suspicion of American involvement. In Cambodia a plot to overthrow Prince Sihanouk was discovered, but not before it was discovered that the finger prints of the CIA were all over the plot. Increasingly, civilian agents from American security services took more active roles in the military operations and in advising the Vietnamese government on how best to suppress the native insurrection spilling over from the north.

As President Eisenhower was leaving office he communicated with the newly-elected Kennedy that Laos was in crisis and that Vietnam was not far behind. As President, Kennedy declared that the United States favored independence for Laos, while dealing with his own crisis of the aftermath of the attempt to assist Cuban rebels to overthrow Castro. In an effort objectively to assess blame for the tragedy only ninety miles off American shores, the young President commissioned two study groups of experts, one drawn from inside the government and the other from the outside. Both groups reported that the political misuse of intelligence and subsequent unsound policy was to blame, and that should have been a warning bell that the United States was at risk of making the same mistakes in Vietnam. The United States did succeed in the main confrontation with the Soviet Union regarding Cuba, but it did not fare so well in dealing with the Soviet and Chinese proxies in Southeast Asia.

In June, 1961, Kennedy met Premier Kruschchev in Vienna for what was supposed to be a general clearing of the air. Instead, the Russian leader ate the young President's lunch precisely because the latter had gone to Vienna unprepared to argue the American case in foreign affairs. That is one of the principal weaknesses of personal diplomacy; if one does not win outright, one loses.

The next year, 1962, witnessed the most serious confrontation of the Cold War. By masterful strategic planning and by being better prepared than at Vienna, Kennedy stared down the Russians and forced them to remove the offensive missiles from Cuba. Americans never knew how close the world came to a nuclear exchange until the crisis had passed; neither did the Russian people. Obviously, that confrontation appeared to have little to do with Vietnam, but actually it was a part of a whole. During the Cuban crisis Kennedy grasped the essential truth that for American nuclear power to count he had to be prepared to use it. Neither side entered the fray prepared to back down, but the Russians blinked first. In Vietnam, the Russians knew that the United States was not prepared to use nuclear weapons, and that placed the entire American strategy at risk. The first rule in the use of military power in support of foreign policy is that one must be prepared to take whatever risks are needed to secure vital national interests. If such interests are not immediately involved, policy depends upon diplomacy or limited military force to secure outcomes. American public opinion would probably not have tolerated the use of nuclear weapons to secure our goals in Vietnam, and the Communist world knew it. It is a simple fact that a democracy goes to war only when there is no other choice, and even then its options are limited to those its citizens are willing to accept and support.

In 1962 there was a sea change in the role of the United States in Vietnam. First, the American Military Assistance Command (MACV) was formed, and the American military presence increased to about

12,000 tactical advisers to Vietnamese army units in the field. It was the President's belief that the increased American involvement would be sufficient to make Ho more reasonable at the bargaining table. It did the reverse. In February the Vietcong were so bold as to bomb the palace of Diem, who escaped unharmed, but the incident proved that even the increased American presence could not protect the civilian head of state. Undeterred, the United States pressed forward to impose its will in a civil war in which it did not hold the high cards. In foreign policy as in poker, when a gambler is on a losing streak, prudence suggests that the player cut loses and move on to protect more vital interests elsewhere. To drive home that lesson not learned, early in 1963 South Vietnamese units lost a pitched battle at Ap Bac. Soon Ho Chi Minh and Chinese President Liu Shaoji issued a joint statement denouncing "revisionism," by which they meant "the Russian moon in setting and the Chinese sun is rising on destiny." The American public was also treated to the spectacle of Vietnamese Buddist monks immolating themselves to call attention to the plight of their country.

Events in Vietnam continued to spiral downward. Over the back fence, American military leaders were informed by friendly units within the Vietnamese leadership that dissidents planned to kill Diem. That was perceived as a serious blow to American prestige. President Kennedy sent Henry Cabot Lodge, Jr., as his emissary in Saigon and declared strong support for Diem and condemnation for the rebellious generals. When things became even more unstable, Kennedy changed course and publicly criticized Diem as being too repressive and out of touch with the Vietnamese population. By fall of that year dissident military leaders captured and murdered both Diem and his lieutenant, Nhu. Then on November 22 Kennedy himself was assassinated in Dallas and was succeeded by Lyndon Johnson. Those tragedies had a direct bearing on the American stance in Vietnam because Johnson was not prepared to preside over an American defeat. Not only was his personal pride involved, but he was at pains to prove that a Democratic President could be as tough on international Communism, thereby expecting to blunt Republican criticism.

A cabal of rebellious generals led by Ngugen Khanh early in 1964 seized power in Vietnam, arrested several army officers who were not members of the cabal, and allowed Minh to retain office under their control. A series of high-level conferences in the United States resulted in a new policy of bombing areas under Vietcong control in order to break the back of the resistance movement. Even though pursued vigorously, the Vietcong simply "dug in" their positions in an extensive network of tunnels, from which they made sporadic raids on Vietnamese and American positions.

The war in Southeast Asia took another momentous turn in August, when the USS *Maddox* on patrol in the Gulf of Tonkin reported that it was under attack by North Vietnamese gunboats. Two days later a similar incident was reported, but subsequent examination of the vessel's logbook failed to support the accuracy of the report. In any event, the Johnson administration claimed that the attack had the force of an armed attack upon the "floating" sovereign territory of the United States. If that conclusion were correct, in what respect was it different from previous attacks upon defensive and/or advisory positions within Vietnam? In quick order, Congress passed the Tonkin Resolution on August 7, which authorized the President to use all military means deemed necessary to "protect American interests." The declared, shooting phase of the war involving the United States had arrived.

Tensions further increased in Asia with the first Chinese atomic bomb test in October, and in Russia Khrushchev was replaced by Leonid Brezhnev and Aleksei Kosygin. The change was supposed to signal the West that Russia was again ready to negotiate, but somehow it was again misread in Washington. The country was pre-occupied in the presidential election then on-going between Barry Goldwater and Lyndon Johnson, the election featuring TV commercials showing explosions of nuclear weapons. Extraordinary efforts were made to conceal from the public the extent of American losses, while the "body count" of Vietcong forces was systematically inflated. Johnson won re-election, blunting the implied Republican charge that the Democratic Party was soft on national defense and validating the Democratic charge that Goldwater had been trigger-happy. The aftermath of the American election was chaos in Vietnam, where rioters demanded that Khanh leave the country. The American ambassador seconded the motion. There followed the strange spectacle of McGeorge Bundy, Johnson's special agent while in Saigon secretly visiting with Aleksei Kosygen, who was simultaneously visiting in Hanoi. They failed to reach an agreement, so the bombing was resumed. Casualties mounted among the American combat troops in Vietnam, and the government was reformed under Air Vice Marshal Ngugen Cao Ky, something of a flamboyant hot dog. By the end of the year American troop strength in country reached 200,000. Sensing that outright victory was not possible in Vietnam, President Johnson announced that the United States was ready to suspend the bombing raids in return for "productive" peace talks.

Intermittent clashes took place all during 1966 between American forces and the Vietcong, the latter proving a very formidable foe in irregular combat. On a visit to neighboring Cambodia, French President Charles de Gaulle urged the withdrawal of all American troops from Vietnam, but the American government did not bother to reply to the suggestion. American troop strength reached 400,000, mostly draftees, while college students and sons of the wealthy escaped, fueling a growing demand to end the war. Peace activists began urging, "Let us declare victory and come home."

With Communist leaders demanding a cessation of bombing before talks could begin, and American leaders a cessation of fighting before peace talks could begin, no talks took place. Instead, in June, Johnson and Kosygan held a two-day meeting in Glassboro, N. J., and they could report no progress towards peace in Vietnam. Secretary of Defense McNamara testified before Congress that the bombing had been largely ineffective, while General Westmoreland asked for 500,000 troops to wage an effective ground war. There were riots on several college campuses to end the war and the draft.

Early in 1968 another U. S. Navy vessel, the *Pueblo*, while gathering intelligence off the coast of Korea was seized by the North Koreans. The incident had no immediate relationship to the war in Vietnam, but the American immediately concluded that it was another test of American resolve. Shortly thereafter, the Tet offensive began in an all-out effort to drive American forces from Vietnam. When Commanding General Westmoreland asked for an additional 200,000 troops, the Joint Chiefs responded by pointing out that there no additional forces available. While the public debated the issue, Clark Clifford, the new Secretary of Defense, was quietly telling Congressional leaders that the jig was up; American forces were simply inadequate to police an area which forcibly resisted being policed. In Paris the secret meetings between Henry Kissinger and Le Doc Tho was stalled for months, pointlessly arguing over the shape of the table for the talks. There was finally a breakthrough in mid-October, when a deal was reached, only to have it denounced by the political leaders in Saigon. The dove of peace seemed to have been shot in both wings.

The Vietnamese Conflict seems to have been the only war in American history to have been fought on two fronts—on foreign soil as well as in domestic politics. In the election of 1972, hawkish Richard Nixon defeated dovish George McGovern in a landslide, the only real issue in contention was the war in Vietnam. Nixon took the landslide victory as a mandate to "re-establish national honor," and Kissinger was ordered back to Paris to reach a final accord with Le Doc Tho, only to find that the latter had stiffened his bargaining position. In December a resumption of bombing was ordered, and a final agreement was signed on January 23, 1973. Its terms were secret.

Events moved swiftly to their illogical conclusion. An end to the draft was announced, and the last American forces (together with the core Vietnamese loyalists) were lifted out of the country in chaos and disarray. All American prisoners were supposedly released, but for years ugly rumors circulated that many had been retained in isolated jungle jails. It is fair to say that how the Vietnamese war ended disgusted America with itself, shattered its self-image of national military might, and called into serious question the reasons for having become involved in the first place. Those who actually fought did not return as heroes; those who had died were not remembered in honor; and those who survived in Veterans hospitals were broken in mind and body. Those who had demonstrated for peace had been invited to leave the country, and most Americans just wished to forget the whole bloody mess.

The Vietnam War continued as the nightmare in American politics for several years, its lengthened shadow being the Watergate Affair. On April 30, 1973, Presidential aides H. R. Haldeman, John Erlichman, and John Dean resigned amidst charges of a cover-up and obstruction of justice in connection with the burglary of the Democratic Party headquarters in the Watergate complex. The presumption was that the administration sought evidence of disloyalty, and had resorted to illegal means to obtain it. The Senate began hearings into the matter with the foul odor of corruption in the air. Accidentally, it was discovered that there was "smoking gun" evidence on the very tapes the President had used to record himself for posterity. The government was plunged into a constitutional crisis, and the public wondered whom you could trust to administer justice and how to right things that had gone so terribly wrong. When a president who has taken a solemn oath to defend the Constitution and faithfully to administer the laws breaks that trust, in whom or what do you trust?

Things went from bad to worse for President Nixon, and after John Dean turned national evidence against him, he no longer had any moral claim to office. In preparation for the end, in August he appointed Henry

Kissinger as Secretary of State, and in November he was forced to watch as Congress overrode his veto on the bill voiding the president's claim of inherent right to wage war without a formal declaration of war. Early in 1974, the House began impeachment proceedings, and the outcome was sealed when the Supreme Court ruled during the summer that a president could not claim Executive Privilege in a criminal trial, and Nixon was forced to supply evidence of his own wrong-doing which had been captured on tape. On August 4, the beaten president resigned, the first to do so since the founding of the Republic. He was succeeded by Vice-President Ford, who promptly pardoned Nixon for his crimes against the nation.

In hindsight, what had been gained by American involvement in Vietnam? What vital national interests had been protected at such a high cost? What considerations other than the "domino theory" had propelled American policy makers to enter the conflict in that tangled and trouble land? When military victory seemed beyond the power of the United States, why was a negotiated settlement not the alternative—which is what ultimately happened anyway? What mistakes of judgment can be raked from the ashes of this catastrophe? Somehow, the most appropriate and memorable words of comment which echo upon such a tragedy are those of Christ when He condemned corrupt official self-righteousness.

*   *   *

"The teachers of the law and the Pharisees sit in Moses' seat. So you must obey them and do everything they tell you. But do not practice what they do, for they do not practice what they preach. They tie up heavy loads and put them on men's shoulders, but they themselves are not willing to lift a finger to move them."

"Everything they do is done for men to see. They make their phylacteries wide and tassels on their garments long; they love the place of honor at banquets and the most important seats in the synagogues; marketplaces and have men call them 'Rabbi.'"

" . . . Woe to you, teachers of the law and Pharisees, you hypocrites! You shut the kingdom in men's faces. You yourselves do not enter, nor will you let those enter who are trying to."

"Woe to you, teachers of the law and Pharisees, you hypocrites! You travel over land and seas to win a single convert, and when he becomes one, you make him twice as much a son of hell as you are."

" . . . Woe to you, teachers of the law and Pharisees, you hypocrites! You give a tenth of your spices—mint, dill, and cumin. But you have neglected the more important matters of the law—justice, mercy, and faithfulness. You should have practiced the latter, without neglecting the former. You blind guides! You strain out a gnat but swallow a camel."

"Woe to you, teachers of the law and Pharisees, you hypocrites! You clean the outside of the cup and the dish, but inside they are full of greed and self-indulgence. Blind Pharisee! First clean the inside of the cup and dish, and then the outside will also be clean."

"Woe to you, teachers of the law and Pharisees, you hypocrites! You are like white-washed tombs, which look beautiful on the outside but on the inside are full of dead men's bones and everything unclean. In the same way, on the outside you are full of hypocrisy and wickedness."

The Gospel of Matthew, 23:23-28,
New International Version

CHAPTER 6

THE COLD WAR

When Winston Churchill announced the onset of the Cold War at Fulton College in 1947 he at once coined a phrase to describe a new experience in international relations and signaled an era of profound dangers to international peace. Indeed, in the immediate aftermath of World War II the aggressive expansion of Communism plunged the war-weary world into a new kind of war—not a shooting kind but none the less deadly—a Cold War.

During the preceding conflict Russia had been an ally of convenience, occupying several million German troops in savage conflict which outstripped in total casualties any battles on the Western Front. Russia had been dependent upon the Allies to supply critical war material, and although appropriately appreciative, even during the war there had been disturbing signs of coming conflict with the war-time allies. Having reached the very gates of Moscow, as the German army was pushed back all along the Eastern Front, the Soviet commissars and the Red Army acted as if they were conquering enemy territory which they intended to dispose of after the war without reference to the wishes of the rest of the world. This attitude was especially true in Poland, the Czech Republic, Austria and Hungary, and the remainder of the Balkan states. That disposition could be traced back to the period immediately before the outbreak of hostilities, when the Soviets occupied the neighboring independent states of Latvia, Estonia, and Lithuania. There were no excuses or justifications made other than the necessity of providing for Soviet defense against all enemies. Of course, under that justification, since the Soviets had declared intent of exporting Communism to the world, the world was viewed as the enemy from which to be defended. Too late, the rest of the world woke to the fact that they were to become locked in an epic struggle for supremacy, which would end only with the demise of the Soviet state. To a large degree, that confrontation was characterized by the personalities of Joseph Stalin, Winston Churchill, and Franklin Roosevelt.

Immediately after each area was liberated by Russian forces in Eastern Europe, the Soviet political commissars established puppet governments, ignoring the governments in exile which had fled to London as their countries had been overrun by German forces. That certainly frustrated self-determination in Eastern Europe, and it succeeded because the Allies could or did not not agree to collective action to prevent it. Churchill and the British political leaders warned of the danger, but American policy makers were more sanguine of Russian co-operation in the post-war world—and Russia took advantage of the division. Granted that it would have been difficult to imagine American wartime leadership so calculating as to anticipate post-war circumstances and political dispositions, the war was planned and conducted in a fog of idealism in which all those fighting totalitarianism were given the benefit of doubt respecting any secret post-war ambitions. While not a subject of popular discussion, many American leaders privately wondered why Hitler, had he been a totally rational leader, did not sue for a negotiated settlement instead of condemning Germany to total ruin in abject surrender. The Swiss or the Swedes would have gladly undertaken the role as mediator. But the sudden shift from wartime idealism to post-war realism respecting Soviet intentions gave America a severe shock in which the United States perceived itself as being under siege abroad and threatened by treason at home. It was a time of palpable fear, fear to some considerable degree deliberately fanned for partisan political advantage. Those political leaders who played that game have a lot of explaining to do before the Great Judge of History and to the American people. Fear mongering is an even more dangerous commodity when it is home-grown rather than imported from abroad. After being recognized for what is was, the Cold War was thought to be a permanent condition, so much the better for those who schemed to use it to overcome domestic opposition.

Although preliminary confrontations of the Cold War took place in many areas, Germany was the first and principal cockpit. As it had been agreed upon at the Yalta Conference, Hitler's Germany was divided into four zones of occupation, with the Russians retaining the eastern half of the country, thus cutting off jointly-controlled Berlin from the West.

That possibility, alone, should have suggested to the post-war planners at least a logistical problem, but in their haste and idealism it did not occur. Instead, Communist East Germany evolved parallel with the free Federal Republic of Germany. In time, the Russians used strong-arm tactics to muscle the Allies out of Berlin if not out of Germany altogether. That resulted in the need to supply Berlin by airlift, and that destroyed any lingering hope or pretense of cooperation between the West and Russia. West Germany under Chancellor Conrad Adenauer was a model of decorum if not courage in the face of adversity, and Berlin was able to sweat out its isolation.

Before Germany could be set on the road to becoming a model, free democracy and an economic powerhouse of the West, basic policy regarding the former enemy had to be established. Both Russia and France feared a resurgent Deutschland, while Britain and America wished speedily to move Germany towards being politically and economically rebuilt. In order to resolve those obstacles, America itself had to give assurances that she would not retreat into isolation as it had in World War I. Secretary of States James Byrnes gave such assurance to Stalin in 1945 when he assured the Russian dictator in the Big Four Treaty guaranteeing the reconstitution of Germany—with America paying for it if necessary. Never since then has the United States had the option of isolationism as a basic foreign policy. The American occupation of Germany, which still effectively exists, does so as a defense against Communist subversion rather than as insurance against resurgent Nazism. Thereafter, Russia's plans to subvert all of Germany having been frustrated, she dug in her heels to prevent German unification, even going to the extent of building the Berlin Wall to prevent it.

Brynes was succeeded in 1946 by the stately and wise George C. Marshall, recently retired from the post of Chief of Staff of the world's largest army to become Secretary of State (and Peace) of the world's economic and political powerhouse. That the United States did not fall into a shooting war in this dangerous period is a tribute to his statesmanship. He kept the vital interests of the United States foremost in guiding through a hosts of incidents. Of his American critics, only Joseph McCarthy was fool enough to call George Marshall a fool and a knave.

First in Austria and then in Poland, Marshall outwitted the Soviets in their own back yard in securing their agreement to the mildest forms of Communism they would tolerate, which permitted freedom to bubble just under the surface, ready to break to the surface whenever conditions improved. Under the active watchfulness of Marshall, freedom was never fully extinguished in Eastern Europe, and with the indomitable will of the people an underground democracy steadily grew in strength. Behind the Iron Curtain, America enjoyed the warmth and support of the oppressed people. There is an important object lesson here. If there is to be an outward reach of American democracy, it should be in a form to encourage oppressed peoples to find their own way towards democracy rather than imposing the specific American version. It is perhaps a blessing in disguise that the United States was not then in a position more aggressively to export democracy as several radical groups urged.

The Cold War was perhaps the most ideological of conflicts the United States has ever been involved in. It polarized, politicized, and polluted the process of making foreign policy, and even more dangerously, it undercut the necessity that there should even be a comprehensive policy established rather than "taking advantage of" ad hoc opportunities. One of the key elements of American foreign policy during this period was that of "containment," by which the United States defined all nations as either "for us" or "against us," thereby leading to a dangerous isolation in the aftermath. The author of the policy, George Kennan, is also responsible for the damage cause by the policy. Stripped to its essential elements, containment required that America follow a "long-term, patient but firm and vigilant containment of Russian expansive tendencies." He also wrote that the United States must use counterforce "at a series of constantly shifting geographical and political points, corresponding to the shifts and maneuvers of Soviet policy." The goal of containment was to neutralize Russian or Communist expansionism. What were the ultimate results, objectively measured?

Containment has been politically validated as a successful policy because the Soviets were ultimately overcome, but it may also be the case that it was doomed to failure, whether or not counterforce had been applied. At any rate, the former recipients of American counterforce are still bruising from its application. It is instructive to observe that they perceive it to have been an example of American bullying applied long after whatever threat the Soviets may have posed had passed beyond the critical stage. Thousands of former high-ranking Russian military officers motivated by patriotism harbor ill-will against American foreign policy as a form of imperialism practiced against the world at large. In foreign policy as in domestic politics, perceptions are often as important as reality itself. It ill serves a nation to perceive itself as more powerful than it actually is, especially when it results in frustration after perceived policy failures. As another example of perception vs. reality in actually overcoming the Russian threat in the Cold War, the American public does not fully understand the role played in simply outspending the Russians in military preparedness, thereby undermining the Russian civilian economy. *Perestroika* and *glasnost* were not the direct results of American counterforce; they were largely the consequences of Russian economic bankruptcy.

It is not suggested that the extent and determined application of American military force did not play a role in checking Russian and Communist expansionism. The American public and war planners were focused for more than twenty years on the problem of defending Germany from being overrun by the Red Army, thereby supposedly preventing the initial loss of Western Europe in World War III. An equally important threat which was not foremost in the public eye was the equally-serious problem of defending Scandinavia—especially Norway, Sweden, and Finland—from the expected early Russian thrust into that area and the subsequent flanking attack upon Western Europe. Both regions, Germany and Scandinavia, were areas in the strategic chess game in which both sides played to win against the other by bringing to bear or having superior force in place. While defense of Germany was the role of the U. S. Army and NATO's inferior ground forces, defense of Scandinavia rested upon the perceived superiority of the U. S. Navy and its NATO allies (also carrying the burden of keeping open to sea lanes to Europe). In the Norwegian Sea, the Navy was concerned about the actual or potential concentration of Soviet power in the Murmansk-Archangel complex superior to that which could be maintained on station in the area to counter it. For years the Navy clamored for increasing the 15-carrier force structure, because the Russians had the advantage in time and space factors by flying multiple sorties by the same planes within a given day. Given the Soviet penchant for practicing standard procedure until it became second nature, the multiple Russian fleet exercises annually held in the Norwegian Sea provided an insight as to how they proposed to launch an attack in the area as the opening of World War III. Similar ground exercises of the Red Army provided a blue print on how its expected to overrun NATO defenses in the Fulda Gap in Germany. Neither American nor Russian public opinion understood how problematic were the outcome of actual hostilities. The leadership on both sides did understand the likely outcomes, which were not necessarily favorable to the West. The consideration is that which prevented Russia from taking advantage was the disparity in the mutual damage each side was capable of inflicting and sustaining. Russia expected to use nuclear force as a normal part of its arsenal of power; the United States expected to use it only as a retaliation against the weapon being first used against it. Had the exchange actually taken place, Russia would have enjoyed the advantage. It was not the military chess board on which the Cold War was fought and won, ultimately it was the Russian economy which buckled under the strain.

The admirals and generals may have erroneously fooled themselves that they solved and overcame the Russian threat because it simply disappeared with the demise of the Soviet state in 1987. Norway, Germany, and Western Europe certainly breathed a sigh of relief, and many military medals were awarded for winning the Cold War when the secret of success it may lie in the laborious analysis of the failing Soviet economy. *Peristroyka* and *glassnost* may well have been more effective in toppling Soviet military might than Western military counterforce. That conclusion is given additional credence by the point that President Reagan could not, or should not, have trusted the Russians to abide by nuclear arms reductions agreements unless the inefficiency and corruption within the Soviet system had not already been well documented by intelligence. But that sound conclusion of judgment is lost upon some super patriots whose ammunition is bluster instead of bullets. One need to go no further than dialing to the typical radio talk show to gauge the depth of what passes for thought on matters of national security. Yet, these commentators and their listeners vote, and they also influence the making of foreign policy.

As stated elsewhere in these pages, the goal here is to promote intelligent analysis and sound judgment in creating American foreign policy, not self-congratulation on how essentially *lucky* America has been or how effective its military might in the Cold War. It is sobering and instructive to recall how close the United States came to actual conflict during the Cuban missile crisis. As the nation prepared for a nuclear exchange, it was the inspired efforts of an American journalist and a low-level Russian embassy officer who found a way out of a blind alley which was leading straight into a nuclear war.

Shifting to another time and place, the Cold War also once threatened to engulf the Western Hemisphere by a native-grown variety of Communism appearing in a country deemed too close to American shores to tolerate. Little thought was given to why any—*ism*, Communist or otherwise, took root and flourished in Nicaragua. Little thought was given to what was in the best interests of the Nicaraguan people, or how that could be served by bringing into congruence with the best interests of the American people. What actually happened in that crisis was that an American admiral, while serving as the National Security Adviser to the President, was guilty of the following crimes and misdemeanors: he lied to the President and to the American people regarding the origin and magnitude of the problem; he permitted his uniformed deputy to collect, control, and spend millions of dollars of unaccounted for private funds in an illegal effort to solve the threat extra-legally and extra-constitutionally; and finally, he coordinated a complicated and illegal scheme to run an end-run around inconvenient law by securing the declaration of a national security emergency which did not need to be declared to justify the illegal series of acts under its cover.

The President involved escaped being impeached because he was an amiable folk hero and because he was able to employ the legalistic formula, "To the best of my knowledge and belief, I do not recall violating the law." The law at this level of policy and responsibility has no provision for failure to remember.

Among the real heroes of winning the Cold War may have been the unsung, non-partisan intelligence and policy analysts who, because of the classified nature of their service, could not invite public attention to themselves and their activities. There were those on both sides who exercised great ingenuity and worked assiduously to discover the strengths and weaknesses of the other side and who provided the dependable compass of fact upon which sound policy could be based. Others secretly traveled to remote places to negotiate on a personal and private level, to find common ground so that the political leaders could later responsibly ratify political agreements with consequences so vast that it will require the unfolding of history fully to understand what they accomplished. These were the heroes who also served by keeping their mouths shut. In the aftermath of the Cold Ware it is sweet irony that many of those who previously played the deadly game of chess subsequently have come to visit with and admire their counterparts for their devotion to country in a way which made it possible to co-operate in the resolution of conflicts even if they can never receive public recognition for their service. To those chosen few, a citation reading, "For distinguished contributions to the national security of the United States," is all the more sweet because only those who have a need to know, can know.

In the immediate post-war years while the Cold War was raging, the United Nations itself became one of the many battlegrounds. Americans initially were proud to host the headquarters of the world organization created to preserve world peace, but as its effectiveness was steadily undermined by the Russian abuse of the veto, some Americans became cynical about its impotence or assigned ulterior and anti-American motives to the organization. Some Americans even delighted in chanting the slogan, "Get America out of the U. N., and the U. N. out of America!"

However difficult it has been to reach even minimal cooperation in keeping the peace through the United Nations, it has been even more difficult to secure international agreements on reduction of nuclear armaments. The United States and Russia early on had enough atomic and nuclear weapons to destroy the civilized world several times over, yet they both continued to build as mutual deterrents. Who could see the movie, "On the Beach," and not be moved to tears of frustration and hopelessness. The plot was simply the moving story of an American nuclear submarine visiting Australia when the madness of nuclear warfare overtook the world. With only a few months of life left to enjoy before the onset of the nuclear winter, the crew took a vote and elected to have their captain cast off to sea, to end their lives in the ocean depths because, like the evocative title of Thomas Wolf's masterpiece, *You Can't Go Home Again*. So leaving behind the last warm and tender reminders of their humanity, the warriors of peace slipped beneath the waves to oblivion. Surely, the God of Creation does not intend his handiwork to end so pointlessly. Nor does American security have to purchased at the cost of daring an enemy to start the nuclear World War III.

NATO is also a creature of the Cold War, brought forth for the convenience of the West in training and exercising the Allies to defend against Russia. Yet, it can be debated, and it is not at all certain, that NATO "saved" Europe from Communism, but it certainly has not failed to serve the purposes of elections in which congressmen win but cannot satisfactorily explain to the voting public how to recognize the good guys from the bad. It is a rare senior military officer who has not profited from such considerations of policy related to the Cold War. It is the genius of the American constitutional system that it produces and calls forth those who serve as effectively in peace as in war.

The Cold War is important in the study of incidents in which foreign affairs were used to advance partisan political purposes. It was a period in which American power in war was invincible, yet in peace or quasi-war it appeared impotent. That seemed to be understandable only by the operation of some plot or undercover activity by un-American forces. It was only a short step from these frustrations to charging opposing parties with treason and the finding of conspiracy underlying every foreign policy effort which came short of achieving its aims. It was a dangerous period in American diplomacy, not only because the problems seemed to be insoluble but also because Americans perfected the black art of politicizing the making of foreign policy. The underlying reasons for foreign policy successes and failures of the period are often still locked in the secret archives, and thus the full record on which to evaluate results is not yet available for historical analysis and informed public debate. Not really *knowing* what happened and why, anyone is free to charge any great crime against the national interests without any real consequences. Those who were on the inside when the policies were created usually have to hold their silence, to be judged as successes or failures long after their demise. And even then judgment of history is not always correct or final.

Great international contests always seem to call forth great effort by poets to speak of our great losses, to celebrate national triumphs, or to curse those who had mislead in the name of political expediency. It is perhaps this very poetical celebration of the successes and defeats in foreign policy which transcends the heartache of the nation called to bear the terrible costs of having made the wrong decisions, or even the right decisions for the wrong reasons. It does not seem to matter whether it is victory or defeat, it is the underlying causes and reasons which call for the vision and eloquence of poets to ease our national heartaches. Great tragedies make for great poetry, and it becomes all the more the instrument of celebrating the unifying victories or defeats. That is the essential lesson to be learned from World War II and the Cold War aftermath. We understand well enough the problems which these conflicts engendered, but we still struggle with the causes and moral questions associated with the conflicts. Until there is a great poet equal to the task, we continue to struggle to understand those conflicts.

God may be in His heaven, but all is not right with the world. Truth and national honor when crushed to earth does not always rise again to prevail. The experience of the same generation which so valiantly fought World War II having to prepare again for another so soon, against a former ally turned enemy, contending on so many fronts simultaneously and with what appeared to be treasonous support from within the American body politic has made the American voter either paranoid or excessively fearful of mistakes in the war against Russian Communism. Little wonder, then, that the mood and ethos of the public's perception of foreign policy is that of a fractured community worried sick over the specter of a dread disease. Sooner or later such concern produces the very malaise which is feared. It also produces a kind of illogical logic, in which consequences produces causes, in which willpower is a weapon of defensive offense, in which tragedy becomes synonymous with sick humor, and sick humor becomes irony. A giving generation asked to give too much becomes all the more cynical. Perhaps the case may be illustrated by one of e. e. cummings' bitterly humorous later works so beloved as a theme song of the post-war generation:

Anyone Lives in a Pretty How Town

anyone lives in a pretty how town
(with up so floating many bells down)
spring summer autumn winter
he sang his didn't he danced his did.

Women and men (both little and small)
cared for anyone not at all
they sowed their isn't they reaped their same
sun moon stars rain.

Children guessed (but only a few)
and down they forgot as up they grew
autumn winter spring summer
that none loved him more by more.

When by now and tree and leaf
she laughed his joy and cried his grief
bird by snow and stir by still
anyone's any was all to her.

Sometimes married their everyones
laughed their crying and did their danced
(sleep wake hope and then) they
said their nevers and slept their dreams.

stars rain sun moon
(and only the snow can begin to explain)
how children are apt to forget to remember
with up so floating many bells down).

One day anyone died I guessed
(and someone stooped to kiss his face)
busy folk buried them side by side
little by little and was and was.

All by all and deep by deepened
and none by more they dream their sleep
none and anyone earth by april
awash by spirit and if by yes.

Women and men (both ding and dong)
summer autumn winter spring
reaped their sowing and went their camel
sun moon stars and rain.

e. e. cummings, 1940

CHAPTER 7

INTO AND OUT OF IRAQ

Subjugation of Iraq was George H. W. Bush's unrealized goal in the first Gulf War; it was George W. Bush's albatross, the bird which in part explained the outcome of the 2008 election of a new president. It is another classic example of how NOT to make foreign policy on the fly. The mistakes, or overt and deliberate mis-calculations, remain to be explored in detail by a new generation of foreign policy scholars, so again the warning is appropriate: be slow in drawing final conclusions until all the evidence is available. Yet, even on the thin ice of partial knowledge, preliminary judgments are being rendered. Viewed from a strategic standpoint, the future of Iraq has already passed out of American control, and that future is not altogether a rosy one for American interests. It is even possible to construct an interpretation of the unfolding subsequent events that the removal of Saddam Hussein, however morally objectionable he was, may have further destabilized the Middle East. That brings scholars again to the primary question: was his regime ever an objective threat to American national best interests? That question will continue to be debated as long as there are political factions operating in the political process, and as long as the whole record of sensitive intelligence materials remains classified.

Why did the United States enter Iraq in 2003, and why was there a growing clamor by 2006 for the removal of all American forces from the country? Is there but one answer to both questions, or are they separate and discrete matters, each having its own series of causal relationships? If the American electorate, knowing all there was to know of the diplomatic secrets of the Middle East, were to exercise common political judgment and were to vote exclusively on the basis of foreign policy interests, would the outcome of the presidential election in 2008 have been different? Were long-range American diplomatic interests in the Middle East compromised by invading Iraq in 2003 or by making the Iraq conflict a principal issue in the 2008 election? These are some of the questions to be explored here.

The main rationale offered by the Bush Administration to justify the war in 2003 was that Saddam Hussein was preparing a stockpile of weapons of mass destruction (including nuclear weapons) to be used against the United States, just as he had previously used them so ruthlessly against dissident minorities of his own country and also his record of having systematically violated the 1991 agreement which ended the First Gulf War. Highly questionable, and subsequently discredited, intelligence was adduced to support these threats, but the American public was asked largely to accept the allegations without being providing the critical evidence to support them. After the start of the conflict, the administration's own Iraq Study Group independently concluded that although there was evidence supporting Saddam's intent, the evidence did not support the conclusion that he constituted a clear and present danger in 2003. The allegation was also made that Saddam was co-operating with or sheltering the same terrorists groups which were responsible for the first attack on the World Trade Center and its destruction in 2001. Such charges were pointedly and repeatedly made by the President, the Vice-President, and several members of the Administration, especially those who were characterized as "Neo-Cons", or those who were militantly conservative and ideologically blind regarding foreign policy issues.

As a purely military operation, the Iraq War went swimmingly in the initial stages. American and Coalition troops rolled swiftly into all the provinces, sweeping up the Sunni, Shia, and al-Qaeda (if any) groups in one indiscriminate haul, but when it came to re-establishing the infrastructure and civilian government, because of overly sanguine expectations from faulty intelligence, and reliance upon Iraqi exile factions who had their own special interests, things began to go haywire. The death toll was staggeringly out of all proportion to the intensity of the military operations; estimates of Iraqi civilian casualties range from over 150,000 to over a million, and one would expect that an occupying power would have a more exact figure of the unintended impact upon the civilian population. The financial drain was also staggering, reaching more than one billion dollars daily. Had the Iraq operation been anything even remotely related to a domestic crisis, it would probably have been reigned in long before the American public began to have questions and agitate towards an end. But because it involved military operations and the sensitive issue of "supporting our troops in the field", Congress hesitated to reflect the growing public unrest, and the war ground on. One of the lessons from the Vietnam conflict was that the public will not support a war less-than-all-out and lasting more than about two and a half years. When American Iraq casualties ran past 30,000 killed or wounded, the Coalition members began to drop out and the American public grew increasingly restive.

The threat posed by Iraq against America, whatever it may have been, did not suddenly spring up. After the first Gulf conflict, the United Nations had imposed several restrictions on Iraqi sovereignty, especially outlawing the possession of the components of mass destruction. In 1998, believing that Saddam was about to succeed in constructing a nuclear bomb, the U. N. inspectors withdrew from the country, and the United Nations launched a four-day bombing strike upon suspected targets. In April, 2001, before the attack upon the World Trade Center, the Bush Administration became concerned about the potential for an offensive action by the Iraqi regime and began to plan an attack to neutralize it, coupled with the purchase of some Iraqi oil fields and a *coup d'etait* against Saddam, thereby hoping to break the leverage Saddam might have against the West. The plans were quietly dropped when the Shell Oil Company refused to cooperate, fearing that it might lead to the exclusion of U. S. oil companies from the entire Middle East. An Iraqi oil consultant, Falah Aljibury, alleged in an interview with the BBC that he had been approached by the Bush Administration exploring several political alternatives to Saddam. He had declined to become involved because he regarded those who had approached him as fundamentally lacking an understanding of the various religious and political factions in Iraqi politics. That lack of understanding on the part of those American leaders seeking to alter Iraqi politics was to be revealed time and again.

The Bush Administration escalated pressure upon Saddam during 2002 and 2003, demanding the end of all production of weapons of mass destruction, a charge which Saddam persistently denied. Through American pressure, that demand was finally backed by the U. N. Resolution 1441, which restated the demand to cease production upon pain of concerted action to prevent it. Still denying that he was engaged in anything illegal, Saddam reluctantly gave in, and the U. N. inspectors found nothing suspicious.

Meanwhile the war on terror, following the 2001 attack on the World Trade Center, was pushed by the Administration—with the full cooperation of the Director of the Central Intelligence Agency, George Tenet, but not the professionals within the Agency. On several occasions word leaked from the C. I. A. that the professional analysts could find no evidence of last-stage Iraqi development of nuclear capability, but Vice-President Richard Cheney and Secretary of Defense Donald Rumsfeld launched a secret program to re-evaluate the "evidence" of cheating by the Saddam regime. Specific allegations were leaked to the New York *Times*, and other news outlets, calculated to cultivate public opinion in support of military action against the threat which Iraq supposedly represented. As background to suggest how a previous ally during the Carter Administration's confrontation with Iran had been transformed into a deadly enemy, several Iraqi political exiles were recruited to write op-ed pieces for the American press. Their contributions to the discussion were generally self-serving and did more harm than good

In February, 2002, a bizarre event played a crucial role in the unfolding story of the Iraqi conflict. It was then that the CIA sent Ambassador Joseph Wilson to Niger to investigate charges that the Iraqis had sought to purchase processed yellowcake uranium needed to make an atomic bomb. The Ambassador returned to report that no such attempted purchases could be documented, but the war party in anger for having their plans frustrated conceived the plan to "out" the Ambassador's wife, Valerie Plame, from her classified position at the C.I.A. The outing was subsequently traced to Richard Armitage of the State Department, an identified "Neo-Con." The Vice-President's Chief of Staff, Lewis Libby, played a role in the scheme, was subsequently indicted, convicted, and pardoned of perjury in that connection. In London, the minutes of a July 23, 2002, cabinet meeting recorded that there was pressure from the Bush Administration to "cook the books" on Iraq in order to secure British cooperation in the forthcoming action against Iraq. The British Prime Minister is recorded as having observed, "Bush wants to remove Saddam, through military action, justified by the conjunction of terrorism and WMD. But the intelligence and facts were being fixed around the policy."

In the fall of 2002 George Tenet, while briefing the President, stated that highly reliable reports from sources inside Iraq did not support the conclusion that Iraq had, or was about to have, nuclear weapons. The

President rejected the intelligence as faulty, and it was not shared with Congressional leaders, or even with C.I.A. analysts covering Iraq. The C.I.A. on its own contacted Naji Sabri, the Iraqi Foreign Minister whom France had recruited as a secret agent, and he confirmed that Saddam had plans to develop weapons of mass destruction but that he was several years away from success. Later in the autumn the Bush Administration, not the C.I.A., linked Iraq's order for a large quantity of aluminum tubes to its alleged nuclear program, but the U. S. Department of Energy denied that there was any connection. Later, in another intelligence briefing the C.I.A. Director excitedly told the President that it was now a "slam-dunk" that Iraq was about to possess a nuclear weapon. Secretary of State Powell was dispatched to New York to convince the U. N. Security Council that there was evidence of production of nuclear weapons. Powell later apologized for having been party to international deception based on unsubstantiated intelligence which he labeled as "deliberately misleading." Powell resigned in protest shortly thereafter, but good soldier that he was, he has kept his silence ever since.

In the fall of 2002 and the early spring of 2003 Deputy Secretary of Defense Paul Wolfowitz, a strong member of the "Neo-Con" group, opened an Office of Special Plans (OSP) in the Pentagon, the function being to gather information substantiating the "neo-Con" view about Iraq, above and beyond that produced by the established intelligence agencies, and to feed it to the Administration. Of course, a rogue intelligence agency with a direct pipe-line to the President was resisted. One ranking C.I.A. officer described the OSP as "dangerous for U. S. security and a threat to world peace," and that it "lied and manipulated intelligence with the predetermined notion to support the planned action against Saddam." Later, in 2008, the non-partisan Center for Public Integrity counted a total of 935 false official statements made by President Bush or members of his Administration about Iraq over the two-year period before launching the action in Iraq.

In October, 2002, the Congress was asked by the Administration to grant it authorization to use force to remove Saddam from power because of the allegation that he was about to launch an attack against the Eastern Seaboard of the United States using unmanned aerial vehicles (UAV), not rockets. There was at the time a vigorous debate within the intelligence community regarding precisely the size and purpose of Saddam's UAV units. Those agencies most familiar, the U. S. Air Force, the State Department, and the Defense Intelligence Agency, all agreed that the small UAVs were not a creditable threat against the United States due to their size and lack of sophistication. Despite that debate, open as it was, Congress on October 11, 2002, approved a Joint Resolution giving the Administration the legal power to invade Iraq to force compliance with the U. N. prohibition against nuclear weapons.

As the United States geared up for the conflict which was billed as a "liberation of Iraq with Iraq paying the costs," the potential allies all counseled caution. France, Germany, and Russia all announced outright opposition due to the high risks involved, the unknown political repercussions, and the desire to continue using diplomacy instead. In January, 2003, French Foreign Minister de Villepin declared, "We believe that military intervention would be the worst solution." World-wide, there were protests against the projected military intervention, balanced only by by the promise of support from the United Kingdom, whose Prime Minister was already under attack for "serving as Bush's lackey." The Chief of Staff of the U. S. Army, General Eric Shineski, testified before the Senate Armed Services Committee that to see the projected action to success would require "several hundred thousand soldiers." He was publicly reprimanded by the Defense Secretary and his Deputy for offering his opinion contrary to the policy of the Administration, and he was soon forced to retire. The chief of the U. N. weapons inspectors, Hans Blix, again observed that there was "no evidence of proscribed activities." Undeterred, the Bush Administration announced that diplomacy had failed to solve the Iraqi problem and announced plans for a "coalition of the willing" to invade Iraq on behalf of world peace. The U. N. Secretary General, Kofi Annan, worked tirelessly behind the scenes to head off what he regarded as a gross mistake. He subsequently declared that the operation "was not in conformity with the U. N. charter. From our point of view, from the charter point of view, it was illegal."

The operation in Iraq led by General Tommy Franks, a Special Operations commander, began on March 20, 2003, using the codename "Operation Iraqi Freedom." Approximately 40 nations had been pressured into providing at least nominal military forces, but 98 percent of the invasion force was American. The stated purposes were the removal of Saddam from power, remaking the Iraqi state in the American image, and opening Iraq to Western economic opportunities. Foremost among the American firms expecting to profit was the Halliburton Corporation, which had been formerly led by Vice-President Cheney. Over the next several years Halliburton enjoyed a rapid expansion of contract business in Iraq, most of it on a no-bid basis.

The Iraq war did not go well; in fact, it went from bad to worse. In a short time, Coalition forces captured Baghdad, but as soon as Saddam was removed from power civil war broke out between the Iraqi factions, and the American forces were not prepared for the extent and intensity of the inter-factional feuds. Baath Party regulars, the only Iraqis who were intimately familiar with governing the country, were removed from all positions of authority, and the civil administration floundered without competent leadership. The underlying religious factionalism of Sunnis vs. Shias poisoned all possibilities of cooperation, and in the northern provinces the Kurds were the odd man out in Iraqi politics. Despite continuing, serious, casualty-producing military operations, President Bush donned flight gear and flew out to the returning USS *Abraham Lincoln* to announce "Mission Accomplished." The announcement was as premature as it was in error. Even as the President was making the announcement, casualties were mounting.

Saddam himself was captured on December 13, 2003, thus concluding one of the principal announced reasons for invading the country. But 2004 brought increased violence, as something of an unrealized civil war broke out in Iraq. Speculation continued rife about the evidence of of weapons of mass destruction, the Administration alternately suggesting that the preparation of such weapons had been going on in mobile laboratories (none were ever found), or that the evidence had been removed to Syria (difficult to verify, but no evidence was ever reported). Failing to secure hard evidence that Saddam had been illegally engaged in mass weapons preparation, the fall-back position was that the invasion of Iraq had thwarted al-Quaida in establishing a base in that country.

Even more controversial was the establishment of detention facilities for prisoners of the Iraq and Afghanistan conflicts in several foreign locations and at Guantanamo Bay, Cuba, where is was presumed that the civil writ of courts in the United States did not run. The Administration was shortly instructed to the contrary by a series of decisions of the Supreme Court, and its refusal to appreciate the negative impact of such debatable policies continued to complicate the military and civil outcomes in Iraq. Even after the Obama Administration promised the closing of the Guantanamo prison, partisans on both sides continue to argue about the kind of court and by what law the accused terrorists are to be tried. It is respectfully suggested that this last matter is a serious constitutional and legal question, not one on which the average American voter can make an informed policy decision. Not everything in the field of national security and foreign policy is subject to a vote of the public.

The high-water mark of insurgency was the fighting in Fallujah, which witnessed pitched battles between the competing Iraqi religious and political groups for control of the country, the new civilian regime being simply overwhelmed in the melee. The year 2004 also saw the shame of the infamous Abu Ghraib prison and abuse of prisoners of the conflict; that incident alone turned the stomachs of Iraqi and Americans alike. Several senior U. S. Army officers lost their commands, and May, 2004, saw thousands of Sunni Arabs on a destructive rampage.

Even though the Iraqi groups, under threats from the United States to leave Iraq unless they minimally cooperated, suspended their hostilities long enough to draft a civil constitution and create an ineffective government, the insurrection in the country continued, with more American lives being lost. The situation looked bleak, and a Marine Corps intelligence report starkly concluded, "U. S. and Iraqi troops are no longer capable of militarily defeating the insurgency in al-Anbar [Province]." The Administration was not pleased with that assessment.

Back in the United States, the bi-partisan Iraq Study Group published its report in December 2006, declaring in summary, "U. S. forces seem caught in a mission that has no foreseeable end." The report was highly critical of the assumptions and premises of the Neo-Cons who had rushed into Iraq without sound intelligence and adequate planning and urged that diplomatic and other means be tried to secure American goals in the region. The Bush Administration steadfastly ignored those conclusions and instead announced a troop surge and asked for an increased level of spending for operations in Iraq. About the same time, the Tony Blair ministry in Great Britain had had enough and announced plans to withdraw from Iraq, and Blair shortly resigned as Prime Minister.

Violence continued to mar and characterize the Iraq countryside. The Bush Administration placed the blame on al-Quaida, and al-Quaida returned the compliment. As if contesting one major Middle East faction at the time were not enough, the Administration took a tough stand against Iran, daring it to build even one nuclear weapon. And as if fighting foreign terrorists were not enough, armies of private mercenaries, soldiers of fortune hired by American contractors supplying protection and services to the American interests in Iraq, began to behave badly, straining the delicate state of relations between the United States and the Iraq government. Popular support for the war continued to wane until it fell below the President's own popularity. The sense that Iraq was another "Vietnam" began to gain strength in American public opinion, and most of the Democrats competing for the nomination declared support for ending, or at least scheduling ending, American military operations in Iraq. Under such circumstances, the process of policy creation and analysis was short-circuited, and the American electorate in 2006 expressed their unrest, largely based on the Iraq issue, and sent a Democratic majority to the next House of Representatives with an assumed mandate to end the war. President Bush dug in his heels, determined to stay firm in the "war on terror," while the new Democratic House of Representatives wrung it hands but did little to carry out what it defined as a mandate to end the war. Clearly, a major issue in the outcome of the presidential election of 2008 was Iraq. Barrack Obama, of all the Democratic contenders, had an unbroken record of opposition to the war from the outset in 2003. That record helped give him the nomination against the "establishment" candidacy Hillary Clinton and his subsequent election by an unexpectedly large margin of victory against an opponent with the presumption of more impressive military credentials. Regardless of how one wished the Iraq issue to have been resolved, it was done not in quiet analysis of conflicting considerations in order to reach the best resolution for American best interests, but in the heat of political campaigning in order to elect a given national leader. For better or worse, that leader is now stuck with carrying out his campaign promises, and American public opinion is still divided on the merits of the Iraq issue and its corollary in Afghanistan. As of early 2010 the future of both areas is still far from settled.

The Iraq War and the associated abuses of the intelligence process provided the public a rare glimpse into, and a review of, the collection, analysis, and use (and misuse) of intelligence as the foundation of making national security and foreign policy. Reacting to the several demonstrated problems and disconnects, Congress took steps to eliminate the multiple "stovepipes" feeding intelligence to the Chief Executive, created a new intelligence "czar", the Director of National Intelligence, to co-ordinate and integrate the national intelligence community, and hopefully eliminated the future possibility of such "cooking intelligence" as had taken place prior to and during the Iraq War. It remains to be determined if the intelligence reforms have cured the problems and re-established the integrity and accuracy of the intelligence process.

Meanwhile America's old nemesis in the Middle East, Osama Ben Laden, is still a force to be dealt with. In 2003 he went on the radio to proclaim, "Be glad of the good news: America is mired in the swamps of the Tigris and Euphrates. Bush is, through Iraq and its oil, easy prey. Here is he now, thank God in an embarrassing situation, and here is America today being ruined before the eyes of the whole world . . . . The most important thing is that the jihad continues with steadfastness . . . indeed, prolonging the war is in our interest."

At least on the issue of continuing American involvement in Iraq, a majority of the American electorate seems to agree with Ben Laden. Since 2007 it has been as ready to criticize Congress for failing to curb the war as the Bush Administration for insisting on its continuation; in fact, in 2008 the approval rating of Congress dropped even below that of the President, largely based on the Iraq issue. If another example were needed, here is the latest in a series of domestic political crises aimed not at a reasoned establishment of foreign policy but at the short-term outcome of partisan in-fighting. To put it baldly, this is foreign policy being made at the ballot box. However desperately a given candidate may have been to have the United States stay the course, or to retire from the shifting sands of Iraq, the larger question should have been: what course of action is in the long-term best interest of the United States? A sensible electorate should be as prepared to question the experience and judgment of candidates who may opine that troops may be required to remain in Iraq for a hundred years as others who might promise, immediately upon becoming President, to sign an order withdrawing them all. If in future, such gross mistakes in foreign policy are to be avoided, the electorate must be prepared to debate such issues outside of the election cycle, when they are more likely to appreciated the pitfalls for what they are. In truth, a decent observance of the study and review necessary to accomplish such significant changes in foreign policy may well take years to accomplish, nor is wise policy reached over a week-end or after the latest public opinion poll.

Wise foreign policy in Iraq, past and future, should be based upon a thorough understanding of the details of complex religious and political conflicts which divide that nation, informed by objective and current intelligence, and moderated by a clear analysis of what is in the national best interests of the United States in Iraq as a part of the larger Middle East problem. Critical components of that process were not and are not available to the electorate; they are dependent upon a large part of the heavy lifting having been done before a crisis demanding resolution is referred to them. Given the historical background, it is unreasonable to expect that Iraq will become a carbon copy of the United States in the Middle East. To pose a hypothetical question to illustrate the point, how many Americans fully understand the main outlines of the Iraq domestic political conflict? What Iraqis desire for their future is as important, if not more so, than American desires in establishing a more stable Middle East. The same can be said for Afghanistan, Iran, Pakistan, and a host of other Islamic states. Nor is the United States the only gorilla in the Middle East jungle. In the brave new world in prospect, China and India will be dynamos of power contesting or co-operating with the United States in the maintenance of world peace.

Just as Americans would do well to understand that American power to impose its will on any other country is limited, short of all-out conflict (and even that may not result in victory advancing American national interests), so they would do well to understand that they live in a changing, multi-polar global environment. In the context of settling the affairs of the world, the power of the United States is relatively stable or declining, while that of several other nations is expanding. Therefore, the long-term national best interests of the United States are served by projecting policy which is just, fundamental, and flexible, capable of being sustained in concert with the world community, restricting America to unilateral action only in cases of necessity, policy being subject to constant analysis and correction as needed. What is needed in the creation of American foreign policy is more brain power and less reliance on fire power. Shibboleths such as "the search for peace" (which sounds like wanderers in the desert looking for peace under a rock) will not do any longer. Head-headed, aggressive negotiation based upon established factual data, and a willingness to co-operate to promote peace, is what will be needed. The Middle East being the area most unstable at this point, it is the prime candidate as the area in which to work towards a new and more successful foreign policy, not one guaranteeing the specific outcome of domestic political campaigns. An even more despicable outcome is a foreign policy aimed solely at inflating American self-image, at the un-necessary sacrifice of American blood. Iraq has been an awakening to reality for the architects of American foreign policy, just as Afghanistan was for the Soviets. These should be the failures upon which new and more successful foreign policies in the Middle East may be built in the future. The future security and safety of the United States depend upon it.

There was a time in the not-to-distant past when following Allah meant being marginally and benevolently tolerated, the Islamic faith being regarded as a benign aberration by other religions. We awake to the reality of discovering that about a quarter of the world's population now embraces that faith, that the areas controlled by it possess critical natural resources which it is prepared to use for its own advantage, that a minority of Muslims have become radicalized to launch a holy war against those it chooses to regard as enemies, and that they cannot be ignored or easily contained. Of late, westerners discern precious little love for their fellow men emanating from the Middle East. Somehow, that chasm *must* be bridged to preserve world peace.

Abou Ben Adhem

Abou Ben Adhem (may his tribe increase!)
Awoke one night from a deep dream of peace.
An angel writing in a book of gold.
Write me as one who loves his fellow men.
And show the names whom love of God has bless'd,
And lo! Ben Adhem's led all the rest.

Leigh Hunt, 1838

CHAPTER 8

RESPONSIBLE PUBLIC PARTICIPATION IN FOREIGN POLICY: A MODEST PROPOSAL

"I know no safe depository of the ultimate powers of society but the people themselves; and if we think them not enlightened enough to exercise their control with a wholesome discretion, the remedy is not to take it from them, but to inform their discretion."

—Thomas Jefferson, 1820

The preceding chapters have recounted the problems associated with making foreign policy in the heat of the American political process., generally to the detriment of national best interests. If that is the case, how is the political process to be reformed to enable an informed citizenry to express its judgment on such matters without transgressing upon the president's constitutional prerogatives in foreign relations or exceeding the citizen's limited access to the intelligence which is the foundation of informed judgment? Extreme partisans may see no dangers in the current process, while others may advise giving up any reform as unlikely and improbable. As a modest proposal, some suggestions are here offered in the belief that it is better to light a candle than to curse the darkness.

Constitutionally, the problems of making and implementing foreign policy are almost exclusively the province of the President. Congress has the power of the purse as it relates to implementing foreign policy, but the creation of policy and its implementation is exclusively within the powers of the Chief Executive. He, and he alone, has the power to make or denounce treaties, and to recognize or to fail to recognize governments seeking normal relations with the United States. Beyond the powers conferred by the Constitution, several pieces of legislation make it a criminal offense for anyone professing to represent the Administration, without authority, to deal with foreign governments. Moreover, the President, or officers subordinate to him, have the power to enforce these laws, which carry specific and stiff penalties. While it is within the power of the Supreme Court and federal courts generally to interpret the constitutionality and validity of actions relating to other sovereign powers, in this three-way division it is the President, by far, who has the lion's share of authority. That concept is so deeply imbedded in constitutional law that it is unlikely to be altered, and therefore beyond speculation.

Recently, as intelligence has played a larger role in the formulation of foreign policy, and because it is the President who ultimately controls access, the average citizen is frozen out of the process except in extraordinary situations requiring an abrupt and radical policy change. Without access to the underlying intelligence, how is an interested and informed citizenry to make judgments except after the fact? Even presidential candidates are at a disadvantage in running against an incumbent, because he can ultimately, if temporarily, control what an opponent can know, and political opponents who may independently dig out some uncomfortable truth are subject to violation of security laws and regulations if they release that information. For all these reasons, this is a problem which must be solved by expanding the foreign policy functions and powers of Congress as the trusted agent of the citizenry rather than by seeking to curb the power of the President. Building upon the power of Congress to supervise, investigate, and appropriate, a new function of advising can be crafted for Congressional leaders of both parties to participate in the creation of foreign policy without violating the strictures of the Constitution. The effort would be in the spirit of parliamentary democracy, and the mechanism would be as a revision of the National Security Act of 1947. Certain Presidents have found ways to circumvent the original intent of that Act, but while it is on the books it is the law to be obeyed. It has not been challenged as to its constitutionality, and it is thought to be unlikely that any reasonable expansion would be found to be unconstitutional, especially if a President would be disposed to advocate amendment of the Security Act.

A final source of power in the formulation of foreign policy is the American electorate itself—those who every fourth year actually select the next President. While the prerogatives of the office will continue to control, any President who consistently fails to level with the public, or who follows a foreign policy the public does not support, is in for a rough ride. Such a President is not likely to be re-elected, nor is a member of his party associated with the same policies. While the employment of such fail-safe power is effective, it can only change policy after it has already lost public support. The adoption of the changes in process here suggested are aimed at not only minimizing opportunities for politicizing the creation of foreign policy, but in avoiding egregious mistakes as well.

The National Security Act of 1947, as amended, was a wide-ranging overhaul of the armed forces of the United States as well an establishment of a mechanism for the formulation and integration of national security and foreign policy. Among its many provisions was the creation of the National Security Council whose function it is "to advise the President with respect to the integration of domestic, foreign, and military policies." Subsequently, membership on the Council has been defined to include the President, the Vice President, the Secretaries of State and Defense, the Chairman of the National Security Resources Board, the Director of the Central Intelligence Agency, and such other officers as may be designated by the President with the approval of the Senate. Routinely, the members of the Joint Chiefs of Staff have served as military advisers to the Council. On the whole, the establishment of this body of presidential advisers to integrate foreign policy has been a step in the right direction, but problems have emerged both within certain administrations and between the Executive Branch and Congress. At times, the National Security Adviser, an office within the White House, has preempted many functions of the State Department, and although presidents have at times understandably resisted prior consultation with the Congressional leadership when foreign policy emergencies arise, especially when Congress is controlled by the opposition party, presidents have also failed routinely to inform or ask *fait accompli* concurrence from Congress or its leadership. This has given rise to several systemic problems in the field of foreign relations, and these problems need solution before re-organizing the policy process.

One problem is the issue of flexibility; the international context is now subject to rapid change, and the President, much less the American public, is not always capable of changing policy to cope with the new threats or opportunities as they develop. What the public does not understand it is disposed to disagree with. One of the original purposes of the Department of State was to provide advice to the President based upon its expertise and to provide a range of options to meet changing circumstances. Unfortunately, in the turf wars of Washington bureaucracy, that function has been largely lost to other agencies.

The ability of the public and political leadership to understand the issues involved in American foreign policy is another problem. At root is the fact that the world and America's place in it is changing. The ability of the United States to influence large sectors of world opinion as reflected in the foreign policies of many nations is no longer within its ability or power. For all its military might, America is not loved by a large portion of the world population. The United States is now perceived by many as the agent of protecting the status quo, but a nation born of a revolution should be somewhat more tolerant and understanding of the revolutionary process and those nations caught up in it. While the United States may properly expound the concept of Western democracy in universal application, it should not expect all peoples and nations to agree with that as a universal goal. It is a function of the Department of State to represent the best face America can offer to the rest of the world, and to advise Americans at home and abroad to remember that their nation cannot force its arbitrary will upon others. A large portion of the effort of the State Department is spent in extracting Americans abroad from trouble they bring on themselves, but Americans abroad should conduct themselves with the same decorum that is expected of foreign visitors in the United States. At the level of government contacts, building consensus diplomacy in the advancement of international and inter-cultural goals as well as national best interests should be among the highest priorities of the Department of State.

The building of professional competence, which will result in expanded public confidence, should be another principal goal of American diplomacy. It is an unfortunate commentary that the United States as an infant nation seemed to have been more effective in projecting and securing American national interests than is perceived to be the case today. A large portion of the American public believes that the Department of State suffers from a terminal case of timidity and fecklessness. In recruitment, training, and daily operations, the professional American diplomatic corps should be among the best in the world, but it is not. When the principal posts abroad are treated as plums to be awarded to contributors to political campaigns, is it any wonder that the professionals ask why they should strive to excel. When their insights arrived at by years of specialization in a given geographic area are often overlooked by their political superiors, is it any wonder that they become discouraged, and the

American public further questions if the investment in the second-largest department of the government is worth the cost. Presidents and Secretaries of State who spend an inordinate amount of time conducting "personal diplomacy" undercut the very machinery the Department was designed to facilitate. Give the Department of State—its head and rank and file—real, meaningful, and important work to do and allow them to do it. If the Department needs reformation to enable response to that challenge, let it be done. A priority should be infusion of new morale, pride, and competence within the Department, and as a model one needs to look no further than the first Secretary of State, Thomas Jefferson. He ran a highly effective operation with just eight staff members and an annual budget of only $34,000. Among the reformations suggested is a policy of bringing academic scholars of American Diplomacy into the Department for one-year visiting appointments to allow them to test their academic competence in the real world, and in exchange having senior American diplomats invited as resident scholars in those colleges and universities likely to produce future diplomatic personnel. The result should be a generation of better-informed citizens as well as better-educated diplomats.

The sometimes opposing function of the Departments of Defense and State is still another problem in foreign policy. It is axiomatic that the aim of the former is to win whatever wars America may stumble into, while that of the latter is to avoid war and conflict insofar as possible. The National Security Act has been effective in clarifying and integrating the projection of American power and influence, but there are still instances in which the public quite properly wonders just who is in charge of foreign policy. A cursory analysis of the operation in Iraq will illustrate the point. It was the Defense Department which set Iraq policy long before and after military operations were declared successful; it was the same Department which claimed the right of selection of the American Ambassador in Iraq; and it is that same Department through which the Iraqi government is expected to conduct diplomacy with the United States. Unfortunately, the same pattern seems to be repeating itself in Afghanistan.

The shadow of nuclear arms is still an un-focused issue in American foreign policy, and the resulting confusion makes the accomplishment of international elimination of that class of weaponry all the more difficult to achieve. The long-range American commitment to that policy is clear enough, but it has not yet found a clear focus or leadership within the Department of State. Any effort to reduce or control such weapons always involves the co-equal participation of the Department of Defense. To the extent the Department of State is concerned about the problem, it expresses that concern by suggesting isolation of rouge states threatening to acquire nuclear weapons, instead of focusing international pressure and sanctions against proliferation while giving lip-service to the indefinite goal of abolishing the weapons. Why not give the State Department the duty of promoting specific and concrete steps aimed at the eventual, verified, and effective international elimination of nuclear weapons as weapons of terror?

Lastly, the role of intelligence gathering as it is currently organized in the American system prevents the functioning of the Department of State at the highest level of efficiency. While it is true that the Department has its own Bureau of Intelligence, it self-limits its activity to strictly political and economic data, usually based upon open sources, and the final product thereby lacks the importance and sharpness it needs to have in the formulation of foreign policy. Having State Department personnel serve tours of duty in the several intelligence agencies should hone their skills of collection and analysis of political intelligence as well as giving them a greater appreciation of the more specialized intelligence from other agencies as it relates to foreign policy. Greater responsibilities in the formulation of policy should attract more competent diplomats to serve with greater efficiency. In any reformation, the Department of State should regain its rightful and historic place as the principal originator, coordinator of, and spokesman for American foreign policy.

*   *   *

Now at last it is time to make a modest proposal for improving the process by which foreign policy is made.

As the first step in reforming the process of making American foreign policy, it is suggested that a bi-partisan study group, drawing experts in the field of diplomacy from both inside and outside the government, be appointed by the President and be charged with the responsibility of re-stating and codifying the principles of American foreign policy, as recommendations for the consideration of the President and Congress. Its deliberations should be as transparent as possible, its recommendations should be cast in broad statements not requiring frequent change, and it should be careful that its recommendations reflect the broadest possible bi-partisan public support. Its final report should be the basis of a Concurrent Resolution stating the underlying foreign policy of the United States. After adoption, it should be widely disseminated throughout the United States and the world community, and it should guide the conduct of American diplomacy until altered as suggested below. It would be expected that the specific points would include a return to previous successful foreign policies, an update of those more recently adopted and still serving national interests, and newer policies appropriate to changing national and world circumstances. As the product of the objective analytical process, it should better serve the changing requirements of American national interests. Foreign policy should be a prospective projection, not an ad-hoc reaction. An expected by-product would be an enhanced public interest in foreign policy.

A second and continuing step in the reformation and change of American foreign policy would be the enlargement of the membership of the National Security Council to include both the majority chairmen and ranking minority members of the Senate Foreign Relations Committee and the House Foreign Affairs Committee. These four additional members already have the security clearances providing access to the necessary intelligence, and as members of Congress rather than political appointees of the President they would at once provide a degree of independence and representative public input now absent. The representatives of the minority party would also provide a powerful stimulus towards damping the use of foreign policy as a "wedge issue" in political debate. The President would continue to serve as chairman of the policy council, and its recommendations to him are not the result of majority vote. Adding additional advisers to the President would not diminish his primary responsibility as the principal architect of foreign policy; he would retain his constitutional right to accept or reject advice, but it would raise the practical cost of rejection and promote bi-partisan cooperation in a critical area touching national security. It would result in a more rational establishment of new principles of policy beyond what is expedient to the President and his party, as well as providing an opportunity for enlarged public participation in the process. When it is known that minutes of the deliberations of the Security Council are being recorded for posterity and future public access, the purely partisan aspects of the creation of foreign policy on the fly will be drastically reduced. That is the goal and aim of this study.

An early foray into the study of the process of making foreign policy by the author is his doctoral dissertation, *The Senate Foreign Relations Committee and Foreign Affairs In the Administrations of Garfield, Arthur, and Cleveland* (Charlottesville: University of Virginia, 1952).

www.ingramcontent.com/pod-product-compliance
Lightning Source LLC
Chambersburg PA
CBHW030403290526
45785CB00004B/1890